REST
ETHIC

BE MORE, HAVE MORE, DO LESS

REST ETHIC

BE MORE, HAVE MORE, DO LESS

DR. SEAN ORR

THRONE
PUBLISHING GROUP

Throne Publishing Group
2329 N Career Ave #215
Sioux Falls, SD 57107
ThronePG.com

TABLE OF CONTENTS

INTRODUCTION

You might be thinking, "Shouldn't that read 'Work Ethic'? After all, isn't a strong work ethic the driver of success and achievement today? If that's true, then wouldn't a book called 'Rest Ethic' be all about lazing around and not working toward your goals?" That's not what this book is about. This book is about how a strong work ethic, coupled with a strong rest ethic, can make a huge shift in your life so you can have the career, health, and relationships you aspire to. Most of us believe that hard work, and hard work alone, will get us what we want. When we run into obstacles, we work harder. We dig in and muscle through. We persevere and are undeterred. When things get tough, we work harder and get tougher.

Does that sound like you? I know it was me.

I've learned about the need for resting and recovery the hard way. I grew up and lived with the belief that hard work was necessary to get ahead in life. My parents came from hard-working families, and they were also hard workers themselves. When my brother and I were growing up, they owned several grocery stores. My mom worked a second job when the business first started, and my dad worked endless hours to get things off the ground. Their hard work eventually brought the success they wanted, but it also brought stress and, eventually, ill health. Both of my parents suffered from some of the most common ailments of our current society: heart disease, high blood pressure, high cholesterol, cancer, and sleeping difficulties. Thankfully, both of my parents are now doing well and have their sights set on a much more restful and less stressful retirement.

Both my mom and dad have incredible work ethics, and I am incredibly thankful to both of them for instilling the value of hard work in me. When obstacles arose, both would dig in and work harder, push more, and raise their intensity. But it was this focus on work ethic alone that led to the mental burnout and physical illnesses they both experienced.

I followed the same path. Ironically, I should have known better. As a doctor of chiropractic, I love helping patients restore their health, coaching patients on lifestyle choices, and helping them live more energetic lives. Unfortunately, I was much better at giving advice than living it. My first "ah-ha" moment occurred when my wife, Treva, and I were on vacation in St. Lucia. We hadn't taken a week-long holiday in five years because we were both working extremely hard building our practice. Even with the burden of school loans and business debts, we devoted all of our energy to building our business. And it worked! In those five years, we developed a very busy and successful chiropractic practice. And, like my parents, we had started to develop some health issues from the constant stress. I remember feeling absolute fatigue in every cell of my body as we lay on the beach together in St. Lucia. After the first day of total relaxation, great food, and quality time with my soulmate, I remember feeling like life was returning to my body. I was finally aware of just how numb my body and senses had become. My tank was empty. I remember thinking that there must be an easier way. I couldn't continue this long without having a bigger effect on my health and happiness. As I lay in the sun, reading and journaling and thinking about my situation, it occurred to me that I certainly didn't need to work harder—my work ethic was solid. What I needed was a solid rest ethic.

This was an epiphany for me! I told my wife about my new realization and started to read and research all that I could about resting, recovering, and its widespread effects on health and performance. My wish was to actually change some of my behaviors instead of just reading and researching about changing. But my newfound passion just added more to my daily whirlwind. I juggled more and pushed myself more, and although I took more vacations, I kept pushing forward without taking the much-needed recovery time my body and mind needed. It was nearly ten years after my initial "ah-ha" on the beach, and several more illnesses, before my body finally said "no more."

I woke up one Wednesday morning in late June to the birds singing and sun shining. I had just gotten over a flu-like bug and had been very busy in my practice. I had also finished up a hectic time of teaching and travelling to give seminars. I remember that my leg felt slightly different as it rubbed across the sheets that morning. As I got myself ready for the shower, I suddenly noticed that I couldn't feel my left thigh. I continued to touch and check my leg, and I noticed that my left glute was also feeling numb. Thinking that I may be developing a low-back disc problem, I continued with my shower. As I lathered the soap up on my body, I also noticed with some surprise that I couldn't feel my left arm, shoulder, or my side. Toweling off, it felt like my whole left side belonged to someone else. I was very aware I was touching the areas but couldn't feel where I was touching. It was very concerning for me, but being the driven person I was, I got changed and headed off to work. In my mind, I didn't want to let my patients or staff down by cancelling a very busy day. And in my over-optimistic, delusional way, I believed that once I got moving, everything would start to feel better. It didn't. By lunch time, the numbness had intensified and had progressed up my neck. I cancelled my afternoon and headed to the hospital.

The Emergency Department nurse moved me immediately in to see the ER doctor on call. The doctor went through a complete neurological and cardiac exam, followed by a CT scan to rule out a heart problem or stroke. Thankfully, I wasn't suffering from a stroke, but the doctor was still unsure of the cause of my symptoms. I was referred to the emergency neuro clinic in a city near my home and saw a terrific neurologist. After her workup and subsequent MRI, I was diagnosed with demyelinating lesions secondary to a viral infection in my brain and spinal cord. Fortunately, the lesions where very small. The neurologist felt that my condition would improve in time, but I would require rest. Rest indeed. I had to take the next two months off of work and hired a locum doctor to fill in while I recovered. It took nearly two years for me to finally have no symptoms in my arm and leg, and to this day I have to watch my energy expenditures. Although I am feeling better and exercising regularly, I still have to be diligent and disciplined in my self-care to ensure I'm feeling my best. This illness has been both my biggest challenge and my biggest blessing, and it is the main reason I wanted to complete this book.

Today, many of us live the same hectic, sometimes maniacal pace that puts work and "succeeding" ahead of just about everything else, including ourselves. I see this countless times every day with my patients. So many people are exhausted, physically and mentally, and as a result suffer varying stages of illness. The exhaustion and fatigue leads to a spillover effect in their personal lives, finances, and relationships. Even more disturbing is that the trend seems to be increasing. People feel like they're on a treadmill that they can't get off. They're in a cycle of stuck. You probably feel that way too; otherwise you wouldn't have read this far! My intention in writing this book is to help people think differently. It's to help people get off the never-ending treadmill. It's to make resting and self-care valued as highly in our world as working and producing. There is a way to stop the craziness and regain your life.

It doesn't mean you have to lose the feeling in your whole side or have some other wake-up call to change. It does mean you have to work on yourself. It means shifting your thinking around your work and your life. It means recognizing that you are your life's biggest asset and that you are responsible for yourself. It means that you need to realize that you're enough and you're worth it. It means taking this knowledge and using it in your life. The solution is to develop your Rest Ethic.

CHAPTER ONE

REST ETHIC DEFINED

"Sometimes the most urgent and vital thing you can possibly do is take a complete rest."

— Ashleigh Brilliant

What is the Rest Ethic? When I explain the concept of this book, people tend to stare at me with a puzzled but curious look. For some, their weariness resonates with the idea of needing rest and they are anxious to hear more. Others, equally tired and unhappy, shun the idea of a rest. "Rest is for the lazy, the weak, and the unproductive," they say. Or, "I just don't have time ... I'm so busy!" This is the reality for many people today who are living stressed-out, rushed, and unhappy lives in our 24/7/365 world. For many, work has become their primary focus, leaving family, health, and personal passions to whatever time remains after their work is done. The challenge today is that work never seems to be done! Adding to the problem for many of us is an overextended, misunderstood work ethic.

All of us are familiar with the idea of a great work ethic: giving your best to your work, showing up early with a great attitude, and of course, working hard and long until the job is done. Someone with a great work ethic is praised in our society. They're considered to have great character and even moral standing. A great work ethic is the foundation of our society and is essential—no question. But a life that is focused *only* on work robs us of our health and joy. It limits the experiences that can make our lives, and even our work, more fun, inspiring, peaceful, and purposeful. We can all experience this balance, not by excluding our work ethic but by introducing our rest ethic.

Your rest ethic is just as necessary as your work ethic. It's really the complementary opposite of the work ethic. Just like day and night, summer and winter, rest balances work—or at least it's supposed to. Your rest ethic is all about you and how you take care of yourself. It's about creating time, space, and recreation for your life. It's about ensuring that you have ample recovery and renewal time and are creating the best version of yourself. Sound selfish? It's not. My friend and mentor Jennifer Welsh calls it "self-full." Think about this—do you feel that you give your best when you're tired and worn out? Do your spouse and family love being around you when you're grumpy, miserable, and generally apathetic? How about your coworkers? Do you feel like you're on purpose in your life and serving the world when you can barely get out of bed in the morning? Of course you don't! Or maybe you're like many of the patients I see: low energy, body aches, headaches, and frequent colds. Maybe you even have a life-threatening illness. The truth is, the only way to show up in your life as the best version of yourself is to put yourself first and take care of you. We are able to meet the demands of our workplace, the needs of our families, and our own needs only by creating time for our renewal and restoration. In other words, show up "self-full."

It's a lot like when you're flying. In the safety announcement, you're taught that in the event of an emergency to first put on your air mask, then to help others with theirs. Cheryl Richardson, in her book *Take Time for Your Life*, calls it "Extreme-Self Care." Stephen Covey, the renowned business leader and author of *The 7 Habits of Highly Effective People*, described this concept as Habit 7: Sharpen the Saw. Through my own experiences and struggles in this area, I've come to know it as the Rest Ethic. Creating a strong rest ethic naturally expands every part of your life and even grows your work ethic. The concept is a simple one, but it's not an easy one.

We often overlook or avoid the concepts of a great rest ethic because a work ethic can become overwhelming and addictive. Working hard, succeeding, and getting things done leads to people pleasing, or having people like us in order to get that much antici- pated "pat on the back." Work sometimes involves what we do for everyone else, and we're encouraged by others to work hard and produce. Yet it's rare that anyone encourages you to rest. That's because in our culture, we see resting or taking a break as lazy, or you're seen as a slacker. It's believed that taking a break kills your productivity. Or we simply say, "I'm just too busy." If you need someone to give you permission to take a breather, allow me to be that person. When my patients ask what they can do to help get better faster, I often recommend "spoiling yourself." They typically laugh a little and say, "Yeah that'd be nice!" and then, "I don't have time." But we need to create the time. We'll explore why and how to do that. As we learn about the importance of putting ourselves first, we'll see that time and care for ourselves is the catalyst that will naturally affect all other areas of our lives, including improved work and productivity.

While work is about the doing in life, rest is about the being. We are so much more than what we *do*, and I believe we are designed uniquely to *be* someone extraordinary. Rest, coupled with work in the right areas, allows you to be extraordinary. This means we have improved health and vitality, our energy is greater, and our capacity for living and enjoying life expands. The title of this book says that with a rest ethic, we can be more and have more but do less. The trick is to understand what those "right" areas are and practice doing less so we can be more. The emphasis here is on doing *less* of the unimportant things and *more* of the things that are important to you. Mind you, it doesn't mean doing *nothing*. We must start by determining what is important and unique to each of us.

The first thing to do is to sit and get quiet. Ask the question: Which out of all of these choices will make the biggest difference for me today regarding my life, health, etc.? Stephen Covey often talks about how we get caught up in the urgent but unimportant things. Day-to-day fires are inevitable, but he encourages us to decide what is important, but not urgent, and focus on that. These things are often the hardest to do, like "I gotta exercise today." The challenge is to focus on what is truly important so that we are not consumed by the small things each day. We need to decide for ourselves what is important. We do this by deciding which issues will help us move forward with our lives and reduce our stress levels once they are completed. It is by sitting, asking these questions, and taking the time to reflect on our answers that help us identify what is important versus a distraction.

Darren Hardy, publisher of *Success Magazine*, offers up this solution: there is only one list to focus on, and on that list there are only THREE priorities. Period. Anything else drains the mental, emotional, physical, and spiritual resources we need to excel in those three main priorities. Hardy further explains Warren Buffet's three-step method for prioritization:

1. Write down every priority, demand, request, and project that affects your time.
2. Now, narrow it down to the top three.
3. Throw the rest of the list away.

That is guaranteed to be hard, but it's necessary to cut out the things that are not essential so you can focus on the things that are. Start with your three priorities for the year. Next, break your list down into "What are the three key things I need to do this month to achieve these priorities this year?" Then, break it down to the week, and even day, so you can focus daily on what you want. Once you have that list in front of you, you have to be adamant to stick to just those three things. This is challenging because we might fear missing out or worry that if we don't take care of this today, something bad might happen. If something comes up again, you can choose to add it to your list then. As the wise Jim Collins says, "If you have more than three priorities, you don't have any."

When I look at a list of things that need to be done (and we all have these lists), it can sometimes feel overwhelming to discern the important from the unimportant. But with a little practice, it gets easier. By doing so, we can take control of our lives. We manage the stress instead of it managing us.

People are so stressed out today. Stress has become a norm, and almost a badge of honor. There is exponentially more available to us today, and at all times of day, than ever before. The Internet, technology, and social media have totally increased our potential for growth and expansion like nothing else in history. This increased access comes not only with increased opportunity, but exponentially increased responsibility and stress as well. The problem is that our bodies are not designed to function at peak levels twenty-four hours a day, seven days a week, 365 days a year. Our computers and technology do that, and we've fallen into the trap of believing we can too. We can't. We need periods of activity followed by periods of recovery. Don't believe me? Think about this: Our muscles contract, and then relax, in order for us to move. The heart beats in order to function and keep us alive. A heartbeat is nothing more than a contraction followed by relaxation. Even the brain gives us some great examples. A neuron or brain cell receives stimulation and activity before it fires an electrical signal to other cells. This is followed by—you guessed it—a rest period (or more technically, a refractory period). In the book *The Power of Full Engagement*, Dr. Jim Loehr and Tony Schwartz sum it up perfectly: **"It's not stress that is killing us, it's the lack of recovery time."** The truth is, we are designed for oscillation, meaning periods of being engaged in activity followed by rest and recovery. Today, we are living a more linear existence. It's like running a marathon every day. No breaks. That kind of pace is just not sustainable, and it creates an incredible amount of stress for our bodies. Persistent stress wreaks havoc on our health. When stress levels increase, stress hormones such as cortisol also increase. Cortisol is a hormone produced in our body by our adrenal glands. It is supposed to peak intermittently for periods of stress and then decrease. However, in today's world, we often live in a constant state of stress, which creates high levels of stress hormones all day. While cortisol is necessary and beneficial in the short term, it damages our health when it is released constantly.

The biological effect of persistent stress on our bodies is now being linked to an array of diseases, such as obesity, Parkinson's, Alzheimer's, diabetes, and heart disease, among others. Doesn't that sound like our current society? The message our bodies is sending us is clear—we are made for more than work and production. We are also designed to rest and enjoy. Doing so allows us to shut down the stress cycle in our body, allowing us to physically recover and heal from the pace of our days. When we do that we look better, move better, and just plain think and feel better.

Our mental state also improves when we rest. Not only do we gain clarity and perspective on life around us but we also slow down enough to examine ourselves and our circumstances, and consider the choices for our lives. People who never stop often lack direction. It's like driving (in a hurry of course) to get somewhere, but not looking at a map or setting the GPS. When we take time to rest, we set our direction and look at our lives from a different place. We may suddenly realize we don't enjoy the activity we never take a break from. When we stay busy, our lives become circumstantial, and life can feel as though it happens to us. Rest allows us to examine, think, and choose. Doing so puts us in the driver's seat where we decide what direction our life can take. Choosing gives us a feeling of control that reduces the effects of stress and constant energy expenditure. The power of choice lies in being mindful and conscious of what is the right decision for you, and creates a feeling of power in you, which creates energy.

The natural result of a proper rest ethic is increased energy. Energy is today's currency. Everyone has twenty-four hours in a day to manage. But only the energized and well-rested have the energy to take full advantage of that budgeted time. Proper time management ensures good use of this precious commodity, but it is your capacity to perform and be truly present in your scheduled time that makes the difference. Anyone can fill their schedule to the max and create a hugely productive day, at least on their calendar. But will your personal energy get you through it? Did you sleep through your two o'clock meeting? Were you so exhausted that you couldn't even finish shopping at the grocery store? Or maybe you just had to have a boost from a cup of coffee or an expensive, sugary "energy" imposter. Managing energy, not time, is the key not only to our productivity but to increasing the capacity of our lives.

Finally, a great rest ethic is about expanding both your life capacity and life fulfillment. A rest ethic is about being; a work ethic is about doing. Our culture today is about doing it, doing it, and more doing it. Our focus is on how you can do it more, better, and, of course, faster. We often do this to earn more money so we can buy more and keep up with our neighbors. My good friend and mentor Dr. Douglas Sea always reminds me, "We buy things with money we don't have to impress people we don't know." Sounds logical, right? Of course it's not! We can get so caught up in the busyness that we forget why we're working so hard and what is important to us in the first place. We are the proverbial hamster on the wheel. You can stop it.

There are plenty of good reasons to rest, but unlike with work, we need permission. How many of us were either raised by or live with a workaholic? It's culturally acceptable. My dad was a workaholic, and though it had some benefits, overextending himself for too long led to big health issues. Luckily, there's a happy ending to his story—he has taken steps to turn it around and get back on track. Many of us use workaholism as a badge of honor, or see it as a competition. I see this in my office and throughout the world as a health concern and lack of fulfillment. In their book *Rework*, Jason Fried and David Heinemeier Hansson point out how workaholics are actually less efficient. They are often unable to get work done in the allotted time and end up spreading it out over many more hours. Interesting take on this cultural epidemic.

We have this idea that it's not okay to rest. We perceive it as lazy, slacking off, being unmotivated, or not being committing to our goals. To break this cycle and turn this thinking around, we need somebody to say, "Hey, it's okay. Take a break." In my office, I constantly tell people to spoil themselves. I'll tell them to go home on the weekend and don't do anything, just relax. They sometimes look at me cross-eyed. They have ten hockey games with their kids, three birthday parties, and a cookout with friends. They are trying to be super-moms and super-dads, but the truth is they will never repair or get the chance to reboot if they don't take some time to just stop.

The purpose of this book is to help you think differently. It's to help you understand that a rest ethic is not just important, it's essential to a life full of vitality, experiences, passions, and the people who are unique to you. Imagine living your life your way.

Imagine creating space in your life to enjoy the things and people that are truly important to you. Imagine how you would feel taking time for yourself for the renewal needed in all areas of your life. But you don't have to just imagine it. It's time for you to "get your rest on!" so that you can live the life you've always wanted. In doing so, you will change the thinking of those around you and inspire them to do the same. Maybe they are coworkers. More importantly, maybe they are your family, or your kids. Are you up to learning how? If so, let's explore the epidemic that is keeping us from our best lives—stress.

CHAPTER SUMMARY

Our rest ethic is just as necessary as our work ethic. A life that is focused *only* on work robs us of the health, joy, and the experiences that can make our lives, and even our work, more fun, inspiring, peaceful, and purposeful. We are able to meet the demands of our workplace, the needs of our families, and our own needs only by creating time for our renewal and restoration. In other words, by showing up "self-full." Our bodies are not designed to function at peak levels twenty-four hours a day, seven days a week, 365 days a year. "It's not stress that is killing us, it's the lack of recovery time." The truth is we are designed for oscillation, meaning periods of being engaged in activity followed by rest and recovery. Today, we are living a more linear existence, and this persistent stress is wreaking havoc on our health. We are so much more than what we *do*, and I believe we are designed uniquely to *be* someone extraordinary. Rest, coupled with work in the right areas, allows us to be extraordinary. This starts by removing distractions and determining what is uniquely important to each of us. Greater vitality, clarity, and fulfillment are the natural results of a proper rest ethic.

ACTION STEPS

- Give yourself permission to adopt a strong rest ethic.
- Create time to actually think about and discern what is important and will get your attention for the day. I ask myself, "If I completed this today, how will it affect me in a week, a month, or a year?"
- Unplug. I know that sounds sacrilegious, but it's vital. It is up to us to take control of our e-mail and texting. I'm not saying it's easy—I have definitely spent time as a slave to my smartphone—but it is necessary.
- Decide how to spend your time. Use questions like, "Is this ultimately going to matter and benefit me in a week/month/year from now?"

CHAPTER TWO

THE MODERN DAY EPIDEMIC

"I try to take one day at a time, but sometimes several days attack me at once."

– Jennifer Yane

One of my favorite thoughts on stress and rest comes from Dr. John Demartini. He says, "We are wise to learn to embrace both sides of life; support and challenge. People have to have challenge to facilitate the birth of innovation, creation and opportunity. Over-protection creates juvenile dependence; too much challenge creates precocious independence. But a lovely balance of both support and challenge gives rise to maximum growth and development." This is so insightful because it pertains to each of us. We all stress!

In today's fast-paced life, sources of stress are ever present. Whether it be a daily commute, misbehaving child, troubled relationship, poor health, workplace dysfunction, financial difficulties, or a host of other factors—we are presented with stressors at an alarming frequency. Some of you may feel your stress level rising just reading that list. Any time we perceive that the challenges we face exceed our abilities to cope, we stress. Stress is an ordinary part of life, and our stress responses can be healthy and helpful to our striving and surviving when handled properly. Stress is even necessary to help us improve and grow. But too much stress, or dealing poorly with stress, can wreak havoc on us.

Consider this: You are walking alone through town after a movie late one evening and decide to take a shortcut through an alley to get to your parked car. Well into the alley you see a rather daunting and unknown individual quickly walking toward you. Automatically, out of concern for your well-being, your body initiates a stress response. In preparation, your body redirects resources away from important, but not urgent, functions to ready itself for a potential "fight or flight" situation. Rather than keeping blood around your stomach and brain to help digest your popcorn and think about the movie you just watched, blood is moved to the muscles. Hormones such as adrenalin are released to increase the capacity of your circulatory system. Your heart races, fat is released to increase blood sugar for immediate energy, and your defenses are mobilized. This response could prove to be life-saving if the threat approaching is real.

In this scenario, your body is responding to stress in the *sympathetic nervous system*. You could say your body is sympathizing with your current circumstances. This process is marvelous and even healthy. But stress responses harm us when the sympathetic nervous response is not followed by the *parasympathetic nervous system* response, also known as the "rest and digest" response. This is the crucial coming-down period following the stressful experience in which repair and recovery occur. The many important functions your body was conducting prior to the stressful event need to resume in order to maintain your health. Our blood pressure needs to recover, our hormones need to return to appropriate levels, and our bodies need to return to the proper use of energy for immune functions, tissue repair, and digestion. It is simply not sustainable to live a healthy life in a constant stress response. However, most of society does and suffers the consequences.

Here's another example many of us are quite familiar with. When you go to the gym, you challenge yourself (in other words, you undergo stress) by breaking down your body to rebuild and increase resilience, improving your health. This is another good example of how stress is not only positive but also necessary for us to better ourselves. However, it is not just the stress that is necessary here; we need recovery time to allow our body to repair itself and ultimately increase our strength.

When our bodies don't have the ability to recover from stress, serious and chronic issues occur. Dr. Brene Brown sums it up perfectly in her book *Rising Strong* when she says, **"The body keeps score and always wins."** Unrelenting stress results in a decreased immune system, which leaves us susceptible to colds, the flu, and a host of other infection induced illnesses. Musculoskeletal issues occur and can manifest as issues such as back pain. The occurrence of headaches, ulcers, and gastrointestinal problems increase. Stress is related to elevated cholesterol, heart attacks, and strokes. Chronic stress results in a lack of energy, accelerates the aging process, and is connected to obesity, anxiety, and depression. To top it off, stress is often a factor in infertility, lowers the sex drive, and decreases libido. In short, not handling your stress will make you sick, more tired, look older, get fatter, and have less sex. Good times, huh?

Misery loves company—and when it comes to stress you'll have plenty of it. Stress is negatively impacting far too many of us. Psychologist Russ Newman PhD, JD, APA, states, "We know that stress is a fact of life and some stress can have a positive impact, however, the high stress levels that many Americans report experiencing can have long-term health consequences."[1] When he says "many Americans," he isn't kidding. According to research published in 2014 by the American Institute of Stress, 77% of people regularly experience physical symptoms caused by stress. The most reported symptoms were fatigue, headaches, and upset stomachs. 73% of respondents state they experience physiological symptoms such as irritability, anger, nervousness, and lack of energy.[2] This is epidemic! To make matters worse, it only seems to be ramping up.

---

[1] American Psychological Association. *Stress A Major Health Problem in the U.S.* (2007).
[2] American Institute of Stress. (July 8, 2014)

48% of individuals reported that their stress has increased over the last five years. Here in Canada, it's not much different. A Stats Canada survey done in 2010 reported that one in four Canadians described their day-to-day lives as "highly stressful." This represented 27% of the population. Another 46% reported "a bit" of stress in their lives. This means 73% of Canadians reported that they had stressful lives, very similar to those statistics in the United States.[3]

Knowing the different sources of stress can be an important first step in protecting ourselves from its negative effects. The number-one cited stressor among North Americans is job pressure, followed by money matters, health issues, relationship problems, and poor nutrition. The other two stressors are of particular interest. While many people like to "unwind" at the end of the day watching their favorite shows, playing a video game, or catching up with others on social media, media overload makes the list as one of the top sources of stress in our lives. Excessive media has also been shown to negatively affect brain function and sleep patterns. The final stressor is of particular interest to the topic of this book—sleep deprivation. When we don't sleep well, our body has an inability to release adrenalin and other stress hormones. That means that lack of sleep and rest is not only a cause of stress, but can also prevent us from recovering from other sources of stress

---

[3]"What's stressing the stressed? Main sources of stress among workers." Susan Compton, Statistics Canada website.

in our lives. It reduces our resiliency and our individual stress hardiness.

Stress sources can vary greatly by individual, and what may cause significant stress in one person's life may have minimal impact on another. It is imperative that each of us know what stressors have significant impact on us and carefully manage those areas of our lives. If we don't monitor our stress levels and make choices to protect our health, we may find ourselves in the over-whelming state of burnout.

Burnout is that place where you've gone past overload and have become completely fried. You are physically drained, mentally and emotionally spent, and spiritually empty. Sometimes there seems to be no hope in your current circumstances. While burnt out, you may be putting in just as much work and effort, but with dimin-ished returns and satisfaction. It can be easy to assume that burn-out is related to a vocation or job, but it can just as easily relate to what I call our "life load." Some people may have only a slight amount of stress stemming from their workplace but might be overloaded in their life outside of work. Financial burdens, fam-ily problems, marital problems, health concerns—these are just a few of the areas that can add to our overall life load and push us to burnout. When we get to burnout, typically the worst version of our selves shows up. Our physical energy is virtually nonexistent, we become mentally fatigued, yet restless, emotionally numb, and socially critical. Apathy takes over as our dominant emotion.

Our relationships can be damaged, and the people who know us best may wonder what happened to the person they used to know.

One of the dangers of burnout is the addictive behaviors that we can fall into as we search for the satisfaction we aren't getting in our jobs and lives. In short, we numb out. We reach for foods (especially salty and sugary foods), alcohol and drugs, stimulants such as nicotine and caffeine, social media, gaming, and television. While these behaviors may provide a brief "pick-me-up" or escape for an exhausted individual, none of them address the root problems and can become an energy-sapping habit that perpetuates the burnout.

There are many benefits to reducing the unnecessary stress in your life. But stress itself isn't the enemy. The problem is we don't allow our bodies to have the much-needed and physiologically required rest and recovery time between these stressors. Stresses of all kinds can serve us as long as the stress isn't too big, doesn't last too long, and is followed by recovery.

STRESS AND OUR PERCEPTION

While some stressful life events have an almost universal impact on us, stress, and our responses to it, are highly individualized. There are things and events that happen in our lives every day that we have little or no control over. However, we always have control over our response to these events. Understanding that we are not simply stimulus/response beings, and that we can choose our response and perception to a situation, is using our emotional intelligence, which we will discuss in chapter 6. This is really our ability to consciously choose our thoughts around things that can cause us to feel stressed. This ability is not always easy, but it is something you can develop with practice. Simply understanding that we have the ability to choose to see a stressor as a challenge as opposed to an overwhelming problem can be empowering. This can lift us up from being a victim of a situation and our emotions, and it strengthens our belief in ourselves and our abilities to handle the events that life sometimes throws our way. Let me give you an example that I learned from Dr. Nick Hall in his audiobook *I Know What To Do, So Why Don't I Do It?* Have you ever said, "I just don't have time"? I'm sure you have, and so have I. It immediately makes you feel stressed, under pressure, and overloaded. It can also make you feel like a victim—like you have no control of your time, circumstances, and life. Conversely, if you feel optimistic about your situation and see fitting an activity into an already-packed schedule as a challenge to be accepted, you create good stress—your physiology changes to help move you forward toward achieving your goal, and you experience more fun and joy than if you had maintained a defeatist mindset. The reality is we all have the same amount of time. We have just scheduled too many things into the time we have. Why do we do that? Usually it's to appease or accommodate other people, to be liked and loved, to avoid confrontation, and because we value others more than ourselves. These behaviors root from beliefs and values of the society we live in, our upbringing, and not knowing who we are and what we value.

Another way to harness the positive side effects of stress is to remember the age-old adage, "This too shall pass." It is important to recognize that the situation is a season and won't last forever (even if it seems like it will), and that you still have an element of control. You can't control your boss or a health issue with your family member, but you have a choice in how you perceive it. As William James so poignantly reminds us, "The greatest weapon against stress is our ability to choose one thought over another."

SOCIETY AND STRESS CREATION

There is no doubt that the society we live in impacts our thinking and behavior in a huge way. In addition, our experiences growing up, our parents, teachers, siblings, etc., have shaped our beliefs and values. Here are a few of the factors that can affect our perceptions and lead to increased stress.

Comparison. Social media has been hugely influential in creating the hype to keep up with your friends and peers. This is the typical "keeping up with the Joneses" mentality that has gotten an extra boost from social media. Not only does it appear that you need to look the best, have the best, and drive the best, but you need to post a selfie with you and all your stuff, all the time. Comparing yourself to others can leave you feeling "less than" and creates stress that isn't necessary. Be yourself, and be grateful for what you have. Don't buy in to the need to create an illusion of an ideal life. Just create your ideal life and stop the comparisons.

Having It All/Doing It All. This concept is in just about every personal development/success type book out there, and it's one I believed until my health gave me a wake-up call. Critically think about this one. You truly can't have it all. For instance, my dream may be to play center for the Toronto Raptors basketball team. I can work hard, eat right, and maybe even have some natural talent that could work in my favor, but the reality is that I am only five feet ten—on a big hair day! The point is that some dreams should just stay dreams. You should focus on having and doing the things that are important and real for you. I often see this belief underlie the health challenges of people in my office. For ladies, it's the super-mom syndrome, where they need to be (in the eyes of society) the accomplished career woman, perfect mother, soccer mom, incredible wife, etc. For men, I often see the career-driven, hard-working man collecting all the stuff—cars, boats, houses, and money—all while striving to be the perfect dad, husband, and friend to his male peers. Both examples are illusions, and both super-moms and super-dads end up in my office with high stress and the negative health effects from trying to live up to this belief. Stick to what you value in your life and don't delude yourself into thinking you can have it all and do it all.

You'll Miss Out on Something. Social media lingo calls it FOMO—fear of missing out. This belief is a spillover from having it all and doing it all. We have more choices today than ever before thanks to technology and our 24/7 lives. This means that more than ever, we need to decide what we won't do and what we will do with our focus and energy. It's a fallacy to think we can do it all, and we need to understand that if we choose to do something, it automatically means we can't do something else. Here is the scoop—you are going to miss out on some things. Choose what is most important to you and be at peace with that. Stressing over your decision makes you regret what you didn't do and ruins what you chose to do because you're stressed and not in the moment. Decide and live your decision fully.

Living the Values of Others. To healthily manage stress and protect ourselves from its negative effects, it is important that each of us is firm in our own personal identity—we know who we are and what we value. When we live outside our values and limits— whether it be a boss with unrealistic expectations or financial obligations that exceed our income—we create stress in our lives that may exceed our ability to healthily cope. I love the line "stress is being who we aren't." Stress can also often occur from knowing the right thing to do in a moment, but still doing the wrong thing. This again can come from trying to please or accommodate others, or by making the values of others more important than your own. Really understanding yourself and your values is beyond the scope of this book, but I highly encourage you to learn as much as you can about yourself. You can do so by seeing a counselor or therapist, or even through a good friend. There are numerous online resources that exist to help you best understand yourself so that you can operate at your peak and set yourself apart from the external messages encouraging you to fit into a pattern that does not match who you are.[4]

Striving for Balance. Regarding work/life balance, Keith Ferrazzi quips, "Balance is bullshit." While this is not a complete fallacy, the way we typically view balance in our society is a little off or, as Jerry Poras, Stuart Emery, and Mark Thompson say in their book *Built to Last*, life balance is fiction. We tend to look at work/life balance as having nice, neat compartments of time for each area of our lives. This is the problem. It isn't realistic to believe that life can be compartmentalized, and it can create stress when we try to live this way. Equally, it can be all too easy to live a life that *looks* balanced but doesn't *feel* balanced. We can't buy into what society says is balance. We need to look at balance as very individualized. Rather than living by society's values, we need to live by our own.

In their book *Built to Last*, the authors introduce the concept of having a "Portfolio of Passions." This simply means creating time for the things that you are passionate about and that fuel

---

[4]One of the most helpful tools that I have found and trained in is the DISC and values assessment. You can find these assessments online.

you instead of drain you. These things might take up the bulk of your day or just a few minutes, and may not *look* balanced if we think of balance in terms of equal amounts of time. This is why balance is unique to each of us. Consider Oprah Winfrey, for example. If you looked at her schedule, it might not seem balanced to you or me, but it is filled with things that inspire her. The same goes for Mother Teresa, Bono, and most entrepreneurs. One of my good friends is a musician. He works late into the night and then spends his spare time at the golf course or on the driving range. He says this balance helps his creativity and energizes him. If I tried to live his day, it would kill me. The key is that your balance is unique to you.

We often think it is balance we are looking for when, in reality, we are in search of creating more time to do the things that inspire and refuel us. We may have one key passion or many. Typically, we are taught by society that we will have one passion or mission for our lives. While focusing is important in goal setting and business, having a narrow life isn't.

SLEEP DEBT

Another huge source of stress today is lack of sleep. According to the American Institute of Stress, lack of sleep is one of the leading causes of stress in people's lives. This is not surprising because lack of rest is not only a cause of stress, but as you will see in the rest of this book, rest is critical to our ability to healthily respond to any source of stress. Understand that this book is about not how to remove all stress from your life but how creating a rest ethic is necessary to thrive in a life that has stress (and everyone's does!). Unrelenting stress robs us of energy and in turn robs us of health, vitality, and life. In the following chapters, I'll share with you some thoughts and strategies on how to limit the energy drains and increase the energy gains.

BALANCING STRESS AND RECOVERY TIME

I cannot say it enough: recovery time is absolutely essential. I understand that this is a foreign concept to most people. I've even fallen more than once into the trap of believing I didn't need recovery time. Using my exercise example from earlier, we don't build muscle or improve ourselves while in the gym. That's where we break ourselves down. We improve ourselves and build muscle while we sleep. We are built to have peaks and valleys, sprints and then down time when we take a break away from the intensity.

Balancing stress with recovery time creates a sense of flow. It's like in the Disney film *Finding Nemo* when all these fish and turtles get under the flow of the EAC (East Australian Current). Life is a lot like that. When we can strike a balance of stress and recovery, we get into that current or flow. It doesn't mean we won't bump into things along the way, but it means we won't need to swim against the current all the time. We gain a sense of ease when we find that unique balance for each of us.

Properly balancing stress and rest, like any change, is an inside-out job. The benefits of doing so are huge. As Stephen Covey touted, we are truly sharpening the saw. We are able to think more clearly, be more productive, and think even bigger when it comes to our careers and lives in general. When we strike this balance in a way that is unique to each of us and supported by our Portfolio of Passions, we experience a flourishing life. What does that look and feel like?

One: more energy. We feel more energetic, increase our vibration, and feel more fully us. We have the energy to play with our kids and spend time with our spouse. I have a twelve-year-old who runs me ragged, so trust me, I need that energy. We end up with a surplus of energy to choose to use however we want, creating great fuel to live our best lives. We are going to spend the next few chapters exploring this important resource in greater detail.

Two: living an inspired life. Like Oprah Winfrey, Mother Teresa, and my musician friend—if we find balance between stress and recovery, and fuel ourselves with things that bring us joy, make us laugh, and feed our passions, it creates this energetic, vital life. We show up better and as the best version of ourselves.

Three: more joy. This is our entire purpose. It doesn't mean we don't have challenges or obstacles. It's a complete illusion that we can live a one-sided life where everything is perfect all the time. But if we fuel ourselves through recovery and inspiration, we have the resilience to thrive all the way through life's challenges. As Jill Bolte Taylor says, "To experience peace does not mean that your life is always blissful. It means that you are capable of tapping into a blissful state of mind amidst the normal chaos of a hectic life."

CHAPTER SUMMARY

Stress is an ordinary part of life, and our stress responses can be healthy and helpful to our striving and surviving when handled properly. Stress is even necessary to help us improve and grow. But stress responses harm us when not followed by the "rest and digest" response. There are many benefits when we reduce the unnecessary stress in our lives, but stress itself isn't the enemy. It's up to us to choose how to perceive and respond to the stress. "The greatest weapon against stress is our ability to choose one thought over another." While some stressful life events have an almost universal impact on us, stress and our responses to it (including balancing our stress with recovery), are highly individualized. This is where our Portfolio of Passions comes in. We often think it is balance we are looking for when, in reality, we are in search of creating more time to do the things that inspire and refuel us. If you are able to recognize the ridiculousness of the course we are all running on and recognize the amount of control you have, you can change the course of history and inspire others to do the same. When we strike the balance between stress and recovery in a way that is unique to each of us and supported by our Portfolio of Passions, we experience a flourishing life.

ACTION STEPS

- Explore your Portfolio of Passions. Create time for the things that you are passionate about and that fuel you instead of drain you. Carve out time in your schedule, either in large bulks of time or a few minutes each day, for these things.
- Balance stress with recovery time by becoming more aware. Watch yourself and how your energy level is playing out through the day. When you realize you're just "tanked," take a break for as long as you possibly can and review the last couple of hours. Did you take a break, have lunch, or just push on through? Ask yourself, "What was going on for the past couple of hours? How can I ride my energy a little better in the future?"
- Value yourself. When you value yourself, creating time for yourself becomes easier. Exercising becomes easier, eating healthy becomes easier, saying "no" becomes easier. It's not necessarily

easy, but it's always a choice. When you value yourself, you can put yourself first and not feel guilty about it. It's not as if I have mastered this myself by any stretch of the imagination. I'm still learning as I go, which is why I'm sharing it in this book—we teach what we must learn.

CHAPTER THREE

ENERGY—TODAY'S CURRENCY

"Energy is our most valuable resource—not time."

– Matthew Kelly

Our energy capacity determines our life capacity. If we want to live life to the fullest, how we manage our energy is the key. Everything in life moves and works according to energy. When we have energy, life is much more manageable and enjoyable. We can handle the challenges and enjoy even more of life's special moments. When we don't have it, we never stop wanting it.

There is no doubt that time and money management are necessary to live a great life. But energy determines the extent to which money and time can do any good for us. For example, if I can schedule my days perfectly so that I can accomplish a lot but don't have the energy to contribute and produce during my afternoon meetings, then what good is time management? If I have significant financial resources but my energy is low or my health is poor, then what good is the money? Energy becomes the most important factor in our life capacity, and unfortunately, we have a personal energy crisis on our hands.

We live our lives bombarded with messages, requests, and obligations that take energy from us, and those energy losses are usually greater than we realize. Meanwhile, to keep up with the pace, we compromise and consume quick, low-quality foods, skip our exercise routine, and cheat ourselves on rest. It is no wonder that approximately four out of every five patients I treat report that they suffer from some level of fatigue.

I believe that energy is our most important currency—and it should be treated as currency. That is, we can make deposits and withdrawals from our "energy account" just as we do our bank accounts. Also, just like our money, we can't fabricate or counterfeit it.

Our energy level is something we're often aware of but don't necessarily do anything about. We've mostly ignored our energy as an actual resource and treat it as something that can be fabricated or "mustered up" on demand. When we don't make those energy deposits into our account and then need a great deal of energy, we create stress. We are asking ourselves to do something that is beyond our healthy capacity. This is when we dip into our energy account "line of credit." We are typically able to handle these demands on occasion, but living this way over the long haul will result in health issues and a decreased energy capacity as our body fights to recover from previous episodes of energy overdrafts. And, just like the overdraft fees we experience at the bank, there is a cost to borrow energy. Our body can require significant energy deposits to recover and return to a healthy level.

Because our personal energy demands are so high, counterfeited energy in the form of marketed "energy" products has become a multibillion-dollar industry. The market has gone far beyond energy drinks and bars and now includes a beef jerky called "Perky Jerky," marshmallows with 100mg of caffeine each, and even caffeine-laced pantyhose (I wish I was kidding! Google it!). How exhausted are you that you need these products?! We don't need more caffeine, and the solution is not found in a product on the shelf. Our bodies are already powerful energy-making machines. If we manage our energy well, we don't need the outside stimulants.

A HEALTHY ENERGY ACCOUNT

Our bodies are incredible creations that are designed to provide us all the energy necessary for active and healthy lives. To take advantage of this energy, we need only to develop a healthy energy account. We do this in three ways: make regular deposits, guard our energy spending, and maintain a diverse energy portfolio.

Make Deposits

Making deposits is a conscious task. While there are several universal deposits that can be made for our energy, such as restful sleep, healthy eating, and exercise, deposits can be highly individualized as well. Let's take introverts and extroverts as a broad example. If you are an extrovert, being around people typically energizes you. When you go to a social event, you might just be the life of the party and feel so fired up at the end of the night that you're ready to do it all over again. You might love the dialogue, the sharing, and just being around other people. An introvert might not have the same experience. If you're more introverted, it doesn't mean that you don't enjoy people, or even the party. It's just that being so social might draw on your energy as opposed to filling you up. For the extrovert, the party is a deposit; for the introvert, a withdrawal. Neither is wrong and both are right. They are just unique to the individual. Outside of the universal deposits mentioned, you need to become acutely aware of what drains you and what fills you up, knowing that each is unique to you.

The same thing holds true for many activities. The first key to have a healthy energy account is to simply know what activities make a deposit for you, and then build those activities into your life. A note of caution is necessary here: energy deposits are not the same as being entertained. An energy deposit is something we do that provides us energy and moves us forward. Doing something we enjoy does not always provide energy to move forward, and may even demand energy from us.

There are a few practical ways to determine what fills you up and to integrate more of your passions into your life. One, decide that you're worth it and create the time. It's totally worth doing regardless of what anybody else has to say. Two, start small. I wanted to spend more time with my son, who plays the drums. I thought it would be fun to play piano with him, but I was a terrible piano player. So I took lessons. This only took carving out half an hour every week to get more time with my son doing something we enjoy together. Three, live it up! Take a leap and try something you've never done before. Explore what's in your Portfolio of Passions and discover something you didn't even know you had a passion for doing.

When we don't make deposits by feeding our passions and seeking inspiration, we run the risk of living a whole life of regret without much joy. We wither on the vine. We are all here for different reasons, and we are all here to experience joy. I think we limit ourselves by not tapping into those things that really make us tick and help us thrive.

Don't Overspend

Most of us are eager to save a buck. We cut coupons, look for sales, and wait to go to dinner until the kids eat for free to make sure our spending is in check. But we sometimes fail to take the same care to guard the spending in our energy account. We often just assume that we will have the energy for whatever the day brings us. We wake up earlier to get more done in a day and don't stop until we hit the pillow much too late in the evening, only to wake up and do it all over again.

Our bodies require breaks in our energy spending. Those breaks, even small ones, are huge deposits. Imagine holding a glass of water in your outstretched arm. The goal is to hold the glass out as long as possible. You may be surprised to find that you'll likely last only five to ten minutes before your arm fatigues. Now what if you held the glass for a minute followed by a twenty-second break? Amazingly, you could probably repeat this all day.

The wisdom of the second method is clear to us in this example. But we can sometimes find it difficult to apply this wisdom to our everyday lives when we look at our daily tasks. Rather than taking breaks, we wake up earlier, go nonstop through the day, and go to bed later. But it takes an actual toll on our health, and the overdraft bill will come due.

We may fear that taking breaks in our days will cost us in creativity or get us out of our "groove." But studies have shown the contrary to be true. By taking regular breaks, our creativity and productivity actually improve. While there are a variety of opinions on taking breaks throughout the day, I encourage you to at least take a ten to fifteen minute break every 90–120 minutes. This follows our natural ultradian rhythms. These are the natural cycles of energy highs and lows throughout the day. During the breaks, take a moment to make an energy self-assessment. Consider how you are feeling, and if you need to, make an energy deposit through a healthy snack, a tall glass of water, a little exercise or stretching, or maybe even a quick nap. If you're doing a lot of desk or computer work, consider the Pomodoro technique. It's essentially working for twenty-five minutes then breaking for five min. The challenge is to actually stop and take the break! If we refuse to take breaks we actually decrease our productivity, using even more energy to produce less. And that is never satisfying.

This principle is applicable not only to our days but to our weeks, months, and years as well. A good friend and mentor, Dr. Frank Sovinsky, taught me to schedule rejuvenation weekends every six to eight weeks. These can be a three- or four-day weekend that you schedule throughout the year and never miss. Plan something that really refills you and that you enjoy so you're always looking forward to the next "rejuvie." These don't have to be expensive or elaborate, but could be if you choose. My wife and I love to do a four-day trip to the Caribbean, or we make it fun and simple by visiting family a few hours away. You choose what renews you, but just make sure you schedule it and do it. It's hard to imagine that anybody reading this book would deny that regular breaks are a good idea. But it is another thing entirely to actually make the decision to set the time aside. We must make scheduling for rest just as important as scheduling for other activities in our lives.

Manage Your Accounts

We have several energy accounts to manage in our lives. All of them require regular deposits to offset the withdrawals that life requires. Over the next four chapters we will look more closely at the physical, mental, emotional, and spiritual accounts. Each of these are important to our overall energy state, and we can sometimes pay too much attention to one at the expense of another.

My hope for you is that you are able to better understand that energy is a real asset and not just an abstract idea. Because of that, it is necessary for each of us to take account of our energy status on a regular basis. In fact, I suggest you make an energy journal. Create a one-week calendar for yourself in which you regularly log your energy status. Maybe you can grade it on a one-to-ten scale. In the journal, include what kinds of food you eat, how much sleep you've gotten, what energy deposits you've made, and what has been happening at school or work and in your relationships. By the end of the week, you should be able to better understand your energy levels, including what seems to move them, what time of day you have the most energy, and how you can best prepare yourself to keep your energy levels at their peak for your best creativity and production.

CHAPTER SUMMARY

Our energy capacity determines our life capacity. Energy determines the extent to which money and time can do any good for us.

I believe that energy is our most important currency and should be treated as such. That is, we can make deposits and make withdrawals to our "energy account" just as we do our bank accounts. To take advantage of this resource, we need only to develop a healthy energy account. We do this in three ways: make regular deposits, guard our energy spending, and maintain a diverse energy portfolio. While there are several universal deposits that can be made for our energy, such as restful sleep, healthy eating, and exercise, deposits can be highly individualized as well. The first key to have a healthy energy account is to simply know what activities make a deposit for you, and then build those activities into your life. An energy deposit is something we do that provides us energy and moves us forward. Equally, our bodies require breaks in our energy spending. Those breaks, even small ones, are huge deposits. By taking regular breaks, our creativity and productivity actually improve. We have several energy accounts to manage in our lives. Over the next four chapters we will look more closely at them. Each of these is important to our overall energy state, and we can sometimes pay too much attention to one at the expense of another.

ACTION STEPS

- Identify what deposits give you energy and build those activities into your schedule on a regular basis.

- Plan something that really refills you and that you enjoy so you're always looking forward to the next "rejuvie."
- Keep an energy journal. Create a one-week calendar for yourself in which you regularly log your energy status. Maybe you can grade it on a one-to-ten scale. In the journal include what kinds of food you eat, how much sleep you've gotten, what energy deposits you've made, and what has been happening at school or work and in your relationships.

CHAPTER FOUR

PHYSICAL ENERGY—OUR FOUNDATION

"You have to stay in shape. My Grandmother started walking five miles a day when she was sixty. She's ninety-seven today and we don't know where the hell she is."

– Ellen Degeneres

Physical energy is the foundation for all other forms of energy in our life. Each of the four—physical, mental, emotional, and spiritual—are interconnected with our physical body, playing a huge role in our energy and impact. I am acutely aware of this as a chiropractor—evaluating, adjusting, and advising people in their physical health. I meet daily with individuals who are struggling with energy, and daily I have the opportunity to celebrate with patients as we improve their physical health which, in turn, rewards them in other areas of their life.

Let me offer a simple demonstration for how our physical energy and posture are foundational. Take a moment and allow your head to drop forward. Your chin may even touch your chest.

Now, take deep breaths for twenty seconds. The breaths likely feel shallow and far between. You may have even felt some strain and shortness of breath. Now sit up straight with your chin pointed forward, shoulders back, and chest open. Take deep breaths for twenty seconds again. Wasn't that refreshing?

Our physical bodies, when operating as created, give us the potential for lives that are full of ability and freedom. It is only when we are unhealthy that our physical beings and lives become limiting. And when we are physically unhealthy, our bodies send us signals that all is not well through pain and illness. This places us physically into survival mode. When we're in survival mode, our energy is focused on the essential body functions that we simply need to survive. In the example above, if someone physically limits their breathing, it makes it pretty difficult, if not impossible, to invest in and receive energy from the mental, emotional, and spiritual areas of their life—they won't have the full capacity to make use of energy from those other areas. But when our physical health is optimum, the bank is open! Energy investments from other areas of our lives can have huge returns. Thus, if we wish to live lives full of energy, we must consider our physical health as a priority.

In my chiropractic practice, my goal is to help restore the normal function of a body so that it can reach its best possible state. Many people know that chiropractors largely work on the spine, but they can also work on other joints of the body as well. Most people don't realize that the reason we work on the spine is to help improve the communication between the brain and the body, not just to improve something that is "stuck" and gives us symptoms. The brain, spinal cord, and spinal nerves are like a computer network that controls, coordinates, and regulates virtually every function of our body. From moving muscles, controlling hormones, repairing tissue to fighting off viruses and bacteria to even digesting the lunch you had! So if there are any spinal misalignments or other structural issues, it can have a negative effect on our nervous system and create other, seemingly unrelated, health issues. These issues have an impact on every part of you right down to your cells.

When considering physical energy, we need not look any further than a single cell for the pattern of energy management in living beings. Single cells create and manage energy through the use of oxygen, nourishment through glucose, and protein movement. Our physical body is simply a huge collection of cells, so our body's need for energy and how we create it is the same. Energy comes through the efficient use of oxygen, nourishment through food and water, and active movement. When we focus on and efficiently manage these factors, we make energy deposits into our account.

IMPROVING YOUR PHYSICAL ENERGY

The health market makes billions of dollars every year selling products to make you healthier. They have designed one-size-fits-all plans and put them out on the market to make a profit. While some great plans exist, and people can experience real results from using them, I want you to know that your physical health is not bought at a store (unless it's food!). You are responsible for your physical health, and you achieve it through everyday lifestyle practices. There are three avenues to make physical energy deposits, and when we take advantage of all three, we establish the foundation for a life full of energy.

Exercise

We are designed to move! All areas of science agree that we are meant to be active beings. Our bodies are beautiful, dynamic machines. When we become static, our bodies don't function properly. The cardiovascular system is stymied, our muscles atrophy, and our physical posture declines. The unhealthiest people that I see in my office are often sedentary. You may have heard that sitting is the new smoking? Excessive sitting really does have a huge negative impact on our well-being. You can still create movement in your day even if you sit at a desk in front of the TV or computer. Try sitting on a physio ball. This causes motion in the spine even while you're sitting. It doesn't even mean getting your workout clothes on or going to a gym. Simply get up, move, walk, and stretch.

My wife bought me a FitBit this year for Christmas. I love it because it helps me track my steps, calories, water, and even my sleep. Consider getting yourself one, or a similar product by Garmin or Jawbone. Once you do, take a simple assessment. Track your activity for one week and see what observations you make. When were you most active? Least active? Maybe you noticed something like one trip to the park on Tuesday amounted to as much activity as your entire day on Wednesday. Again, physical health is highly individualized. Don't stress about reaching a prescribed number. Instead, learn the truth about your current patterns so you can make the choice to improve.

An exercise routine ought to be holistic to be most beneficial. Every exercise program should include three elements: cardiovascular, resistance, and stretching. Focus on functional exercises that build your core, your strength, and your endurance. Your goal should simply be improving your function so you can continue to live fully and engage in your daily life and work activities. Doing 100 lb bicep curls may give you big biceps, but it won't help much with gardening or day-to-day things like tying your shoes. I typically am not a fan of machines or isolation exercises because they target one muscle or focused muscle group while neglecting the core muscles we depend on every day. Additionally, while focusing on individual muscles, we don't burn as many calories. Our workouts become so complicated and dependent on equipment that they are hardly sustainable. That being said, if you like to do a circuit on these machines, then by all means do it. If you like using them and they get you to the gym, so be it. You're still going to benefit! In contrast, walking, squatting, and jumping use thousands of muscles, and while they may not help you win the "gun show," they will improve your mobility and energy.

You may be asking, "How do I fit such a comprehensive workout into my schedule?" Let's keep it simple, and remember, it must fit you, not what a trainer who has never met you says you should be doing. You are the best coach you have! A cardiovascular element in your workout is one that increases your heart rate and respirations over an extended period of time. There are numerous ways to make this enjoyable and not a chore. Consider walking in a park, jogging through a trail, riding a bike, playing basketball or other sports, and so much more.

Likewise, you don't need to be a gym rat to do resistance activities that build muscle strength. There are a host of intensive resistance exercises that can be done throughout the day without equipment and space, such as pushups, squats, pullups, and much more. On the weekends, you can row a boat, go climbing, or help a friend move. The Internet has many equipment-free bodyweight exercise routines that you can squeeze into your day. I'm a fan of Beachbody products. Check them out online if you like to stay at home to work out. Regardless, the goal here is to build up the strength of functional core muscles.

Stretching is often overlooked and may be the least understood element of exercise. While joining a yoga class can certainly fulfill your body's stretching demands, it's not necessary. Remember, your routine should fit you. Again, the Internet is full of functional stretches that can be worked into your lifestyle. And stretching is not a one-and-done thing. Throughout your day, your body needs to be stretched, and certain muscles need to be loosened as they become less engaged during your daily routine—especially if you have a sit-down sort of job. You may not be able to perform the "Destroyer of the Universe" yoga pose at work, but simple stretches like toe-touches, leg extensions, wall presses, and air circles make a difference.

To increase your stress resilience, burn more fat, and increase your natural production of growth hormone (think more lean muscle and antiaging), investigate and start interval training. There are a variety of methods to interval training, but essentially it is exercise that you perform to your maximum for a brief amount of time followed by recovery. It's back to the stress and recovery pattern we discussed earlier. For example, you can run outside followed by walking. You can use a treadmill, elliptical machine, StairMaster, or rower. The method I often use is called Peak-8 training. Search for it on Dr. Mercola's website. Essentially, you warm up for three minutes, go all out for thirty seconds, and then recover for ninety seconds. You do this eight times. It certainly doesn't seem hard the first few times, but trust me, if you're doing it right, you'll be feeling it at the end! Amazingly, you can be done in about twenty minutes, and research has shown that this type of exercise is hugely beneficial to burn more fat, increase hormonal activity, and increase our ability to handle stress when compared to typical, long bouts of slower cardio. In fact, Dr. Nick Hall, in his book *I Know What To Do, So Why Don't I Do It?*, talks about using interval training in his training courses for FBI special agents. Don't worry, you won't have to do Navy Seal training. Dr. Hall uses intervals to help his trainees increase their stress resilience and keep them adaptable and thinking in times of incredible life-or-death stress. Fortunately, you and I don't have the same stresses, although it may feel that way sometimes. We can still benefit from having interval training included in our exercise regime. Some of you may say, "Well it's only twenty minutes—is that enough time?" The answer is yes, if you do it correctly. The days of spending a few hours at the gym are gone and are not necessary (unless you're a body builder). Most exercise can get you healthier and fitter in twenty to forty-five minutes. Remember that when it comes to physical exercise, our bodies become stronger through the process of recovery. You don't build muscle when you're at the gym—you're breaking it down then. You actually create new, bigger, and stronger muscles when you sleep and recover. Rather than marathon gym visits that exhaust our already low energy reserves (which can do more harm than good), we should approach exercise as a lifestyle of providing opportunities to challenge and recover throughout our days. This is the most functional and sustainable form of exercise. When you take breaks from your desk job, try throwing in a few stairs and a set of push-ups, or wall presses and a stretch. Then, while you sit at your desk, your body recovers and you feel more refreshed for your mental grind. Rather than sitting through your entire lunch break, throw in a jog or walk around the block. Whatever you do, personalize it and make exercise fit you. You need not meet someone else's goals or complete their video series—you only need to maintain and improve your own health.

Most of all, remember that your exercise routine must fit you. Don't fall into the trap of thinking that exercise must be a huge commitment and exhaust you to be beneficial. I was there once. I entered into a period of burnout and thought that I needed intense exercise to help carry me out. Instead, I only further depleted my energy and drove myself into a deeper hole. We all have different stresses and life issues that tax our energy reserves and increase our life load. Too much exercise can be an issue for some, but don't stop all together. Tailor it to fit you. Exercise should help create more energy, not deplete you. Designate a regular exercise time at least three times per week, but don't let it stop there. Make exercise a part of your everyday life if you want to experience the increased energy capacity that comes with it.

Nutrition

There is no shortage of information available out there regarding nutrition. A new bit of information about what we should or should not eat comes out every day. Eggs used to be good, then they were bad, then they moved back to the good list, and now they are only good if they are free range, organic, and laid on Tuesday. What are we to do with all of this information? We can spend enormous amounts of energy just figuring out *what* to eat.

I've found that much of the credible information available to us agrees on a few basic ideas. I recommend diets that are most closely related to the current Paleo or Mediterranean diets. For those who don't follow the diet fads, that is a diet that consists of good sources of proteins (fish, eggs, nuts, quality meats, etc.), lots of vegetables and fruit (organic if possible!), healthy fats, and some whole grains/complex carbohydrates. If you eat these things, and avoid simple carbohydrates such as breads and sugars, you are almost guaranteed to have better health. It can be that simple.

A colleague of mine once said, "Just eat what grows." What a marvelously simple rule. And the shorter amount of time and process between the food growing and reaching your mouth, the better. Check out your local farmer's market and develop a relationship with a local farmer. Do your best to purchase locally grown meats, dairies, and eggs.

The truth is, food is our fuel and our medicine. The food we take in can have a drastic effect on our energy levels. Next lunch hour, try this experiment: eat a huge bowl of pasta, then maybe finish it off with some chocolate cake. I guarantee you'll be head down on your desk in a puddle of drool by two o'clock. Try a salad with a chicken breast or salmon instead, and you'll notice a huge difference at two o'clock (and hopefully no drool!). Certain high-glycemic foods can spike blood sugars, cause energy crashes, and create inflammation in our tissues and joints. Pasta and cake are two examples. Other foods, like the salad and chicken, are low-glycemic, meaning they are cleaner burning and reduce inflammation in our bodies. You've heard the saying "you are what you eat." This is absolutely true; as your body breaks down the food you eat into its smallest components and makes new tissue with it. Just think, the breakfast you had this morning could be turning into a skin cell by this afternoon! Amazing, isn't it? It certainly makes you think before eating that whole bag of potato chips.

Portions are always important, and so is the number of calories that we take in. The good news is, foods that grow are usually lower in calories than many of the quick and processed foods available to us, and the calories are more nourishing and helpful to our bodies. You can eat a large quantity of fresh steamed and seasoned vegetables before approaching the calorie count of one dinner roll. And your body will thank you for it!

Water

Water is one of the most overlooked and least understood elements of proper nutrition. Many of us walk around chronically dehydrated, completely unaware to what life could be if we were properly watered. Virtually every body process depends on water, including brain function, hormone levels, and muscle health. Water is critical. Not only is water necessary for these processes, it is also necessary to keep our bodies free of toxins and waste materials. Consider this: mental cognition and physical coordination become impaired at just 1% dehydration. At just 3% dehydration, a muscle loses as much as 10% of its strength, and yet our thirst response does not kick in until 2–3% dehydration is reached. Our bodies need water even before they know to ask for it!

So, how much water should you consume every day? On a conservative side, men should drink approximately three liters (twelve cups) per day, and women should drink 2.2 liters (nine cups) each day. Of course, this depends on activity level, body mass, etc. This is just a general guideline and goal. I know, I hear you now— "I'll never leave the bathroom!" But the frequency of urination will level off, and here is why. When your body does not receive enough water, it stores the excess in various places (one of them being your ankles). But once your body realizes it will receive all the water it needs, it will begin to release those reservoirs, along with all the toxins and junk that are within it. So, your increased urination will usually last about a week or so and then drop to more ordinary levels. I have personally noticed, as have some of my patients, that drinking the right amount of water can actually help you lose weight. This can happen because you feel fuller and eat less, but also because it helps you detoxify and remove impurities from your body. This in turn can help us reduce fat, because fat acts as a buffer for those toxins. Drink up and stay well hydrated, refreshed, and rinsed clean!

Don't waste your money on expensive cleanses without first taking advantage of the natural, free cleansing resource available to you—water! Get yourself a favorite water bottle and keep it full and available throughout the day. I try to have a one-liter bottle in the morning and one in the afternoon. I make up the other liter over lunch and dinner. Try not to have too much water in the evening, for obvious reasons!

WATER AND THE BRAIN

Not only does dehydration affect your muscle strength, toxicity, and overall energy, but it greatly affects your brain. Your brain is about 85% water. The brain is the most complex electrical system in existence, and it uses water to create electrical energy for its many functions, including nerve transmission and the production of hormones and neurotransmitters. Some studies have shown if your brain is only 1% dehydrated, you could have a 5% decrease in cognitive function. Increase that to 2% dehydration, and you could have difficulty focusing and solving problems, and you could see effects on short-term memory. When you're well hydrated, the brain can really run like the supercomputer it is. You'll feel more energized, think clearer, and be more creative and more focused. Try drinking more for even just a week and you'll notice the improvements. You'll be shocked at how good you feel once you give your body what it needs to run at its best.

Our bodies are marvelous creations. They are designed to give us all the energy we need when they are properly cared for, and properly caring for them doesn't have to be a giant task. We only need to know how to best utilize the information available to us for our daily lives. Assess where you are with your current exercise, nutrition, and hydration practices, and then talk to your health provider for suggestions on how you can further apply the information provided in this chapter. When you improve your physical health, not only do you increase your physical energy but also this abundance of energy helps to "spill over" and impact the other three energy sources we will dive into next: mental, emotional, and spiritual.

CHAPTER SUMMARY

Physical energy is the foundation for all other forms of energy in our life. Each of the four—physical, mental, emotional, and spiritual—are interconnected with our physical body, which plays a huge role in our energy and impact. Our physical bodies, when operating as created, give us the potential for lives that are full of ability and freedom. When we are unhealthy, our physical beings and lives become limiting. If we wish to live lives full of energy, we must consider our physical health a priority. Our physical body is simply a huge collection of cells, so our body's need for energy and how we create it is the same. Energy comes through the efficient use of oxygen, nourishment through food and water, and active movement. When we focus on and efficiently manage these factors, we make energy deposits into our account. There are three avenues to make physical energy deposits: exercise, nutrition, and water. When we take advantage of all three, we establish the foundation for a life full of energy. Rather than marathon gym visits that exhaust our already low energy reserves, we should approach exercise as a lifestyle of providing opportunities to challenge and recover throughout our days. There is no shortage of information available regarding nutrition. A colleague of mine once said, "Just eat what grows." Water is one of the most overlooked and least understood elements of proper nutrition. It is critical. Many of us walk around chronically dehydrated and are completely unaware to what life could be if we were properly watered. When you improve your physical health, you not only increase your physical energy, but this abundance of energy helps to "spill over" and impact the other three energy sources we will dive into next—mental, emotional, and spiritual.

ACTION STEPS

- Assess where you are with your current exercise, nutrition, and hydration practices, and talk to your health provider for suggestions on how you can further apply the information provided in this chapter.

- Designate a regular exercise time at least three times per week, but don't let it stop there. Make exercise a part of your everyday life. Remember, it doesn't need to be a chore, and need to be only twenty to forty-five minutes. Whatever you do, personalize it and make it fit you.

- Check out your local farmer's market and develop a relationship with a local farmer. Purchase locally grown meats, dairies, and eggs.

- Get a favorite water bottle and keep it full and available throughout the day. On the conservative side, men should drink approximately three liters (twelve cups) per day, and women should drink 2.2 liters (nine cups) each day.

CHAPTER FIVE

MENTAL ENERGY—THE AFTERTHOUGHT THAT SHOULDN'T BE

"You have power over your mind, not outside events. Realize this, and you will find strength."

– Marcus Aurelis

Mental energy is the "brain power" that has incredible impact on our overall energy levels and well-being. The importance of our mental health cannot be understated. Our mental well-being has the ability to not just affect our thoughts in some abstract fashion but also to affect our overall energy capacity. We are learning that the potential of our mental capacities is virtually limitless; it is only hindered by our own management of it. This is particularly relevant today, as we live in a society that expects us to be ever present through technology and ever attentive to advertisements.

Throughout our days, we make mental attachments to various things. Sometimes these attachments become mindless compulsions and habits. Some habits are obvious, such as caffeine, alcohol, nicotine, or prescription drugs. Anytime we develop a dependence on substances to get us through our days, we are counterfeiting the mental energy our body is designed to provide—and overdrawing our energy accounts. Remember, overdrafts come with pricey fees! Other habits are less apparent, like an energy-sapping compulsion to screen time. Heavy media usage is now connected with depression, stress, and fatigue.[5] Being overly competitive is another habit, and it is often mistaken as a virtue. But feeling the urge to always be first can take a toll on us (those of us who always need to pass the next car on the highway know what I am talking about). Mental attachments can be costly, and they are numerous and diverse. Recognizing that we all have them, learning to identify them, and breaking them is an invaluable process.[6]

One of the most common groups of medications on the market is antidepressants. The usage of this group of drugs has grown exponentially over the last decade. I see depression and social anxiety listed as health concerns of numerous patients who visit my office. Certainly there are patients that need these medications, but often I see people who are down on themselves and their lives because of their mental perceptions. All of us get feelings of mild depression or the blues sometimes. One of best ways to deal with those times was revealed to me by Dr. Doug Sea at a professional seminar.

---

[5]F.A.C.S., David Volpi M.D. P.C. "Heavy Technology Use Linked to Fatigue, Stress and Depression in Young Adults." The Huffington Post. Accessed June 30, 2016. http://www.huffingtonpost.com/david-volpi-md-pc-facs/technology-depression_b_1723625.html.
[6]For follow-up reading: May, G. G. (1988). Addiction and grace.

He explained that we have two perceptions about a situation, the way it "ought" to be, and the way it actually "is." When we get caught up in the illusion of what our mind thinks a situation "ought" to be, we automatically compare it with how it really "is." The result is feeling down, depressed, and generally low-energy because we've created a state in our mind that we aren't enough or that we've failed. When we consciously choose to focus on what "is" and put efforts into changing what "is," we can eventually attain the "ought." This is similar to the "Circle of Influence and Concern" example coming up in this chapter. For example, if we believe that we "ought to be forty pounds lighter," we compare an illusionary ideal to the way we are currently—the way it "is." We then beat ourselves up and feel guilty and down on ourselves, which drains our mental energy. Focusing on what "is" allows us to recognize that we need to take small steps toward losing the weight. We can then be empowered to eat a little differently, exercise a little more, and slowly but surely the weight can come off with many small victories. Eventually this can help you hit the goal, but without the comparison, guilt, and mental stress. I found this to be an invaluable tool and have taught it to many patients when I sensed their depression stemmed from a perception of "ought versus is." Check your own thoughts with this in mind and you may be able to shift your thinking and reconnect with a great source of mental energy.

There is great untapped potential in our mental capacities that we are only beginning to understand. We can make significant contributions to our overall health and energy beyond what was previously thought possible. The emerging field of psychoendo-neuroimmunology (now that's a mouthful!) is helping us connect our mental thoughts and their impact on our body and health. This field studies our psychology and its effects on our endocrine (hormonal) system, neurological system, and the effects on our immune system and function.

Our minds and bodies are always interconnected. When I explain to a patient that their mental stress can be a reason for their inflamed back or headache, I usually get a confused look. The patient usually doesn't understand how a thought can influence their muscles and physiology. I usually give this example: Think of what happens when someone says something embarrassing to you. Your brain processes it, you perceive that it's embarrassing, and then you feel the sensation of your cheeks blushing. You can literally see blushing, and this change in physiology all stemmed from a thought. Our thoughts are continuously affecting our bodies. Dr. Norman Cousins was a pioneer in this area of research, and we'll talk more about him and his own experience in chapter 7: Emotional Energy. His work made the world realize the importance of what and how we are thinking and the enormous effects on our health and well-being. Our perceptions and thoughts can hugely affect the stress response in our body. If we see an event as a challenge, we create eustress, or a good stress response. If we see an event as a negative, unwinnable challenge or as a threat, we create a negative stress response, which can make us ill. Interestingly, two different people could have either response—it is all based on their individual perception. Mental energy is inextricably tied to our thoughts, so we need to take responsibility for how we think through awareness, focus, and mental rest time.

AWARENESS

Self

Firstly, we have to recognize that we have the power to choose what we think about and what we allow to reside in our minds. That is, we have to think about what we are thinking about. There are things that are just not *worth* thinking about. Just because it is on the news does not make it worth our mental energy. There are also things that we simply do *not need* to think about, like reconsidering our fabric softener choice at every commercial break. Having the awareness to protect our mental energy requires us to take an assessment of our surroundings and consider whether or not they are essential. A big part of the process is simplifying our lives. If you frequently feel distracted, obsess on things, or have compulsive habits, then there are probably too many unnecessary energy withdrawals. It's stealing energy from the rest of your life.

Here are some things to consider: Do I spend too much time on negative thoughts? If so, try the rubber band method to help "snap" yourself back into a better state. That is, anytime you are overanxious or dwelling on something negative, snap a rubber band on your wrist to remind yourself to change your thinking.

Dr. Shawn Achor, a positive psychology researcher from Harvard, is exploring the effects of our negative thinking and offers concrete research proving that we can change it. Check out his TED talk: "Shawn Achor: The happy secret to better work." In his talk, Dr. Achor outlines five steps, completed over twenty-one days, that can limit our negativity and rewire our brains to be more positive. Here are the five steps:

1. Gratitude—think of three new things that you are grateful for every day. This helps you look for the positive in your life.
2. Journal—record in your journal one positive experience that you've had in the last twenty-four hours. This activity allows you to relive the experience.
3. Exercise—include exercise in your daily routine to help the brain function at an optimum and create feel good chemicals. It also helps your brain recognize that your behavior matters.
4. Meditation—meditation can help quiet and slow our minds down, breaking free of the cultural ADD/ADHD we experience via technology, media, etc., and help us begin to focus on specific tasks vs. multitasking.
5. Random Acts of Kindness—giving freely in a random act of kindness makes us feel good and spreads your happiness with others.

Try these five simple activities and you'll be amazed at how your thinking and disposition changes.

Are there relationships in your life that take too much unnecessary mental energy or that bring you down? Sometimes changing the terms of a relationship is the healthiest thing you can do. The healthiest way to do this is to be kind and honest. If necessary, share with that person that you are not rejecting them for who they are; you are rejecting the current terms of the relationship you have with them.

Are there spaces of chaos that need to be put into order? Clutter does no good for our minds. We don't work best in the midst of it, and it is incredibly distracting. Consider if there is a place that you have a difficult time feeling at rest with yourself because of all the clutter. It may be your car, office, living room, or even your fridge. Go ahead, take the time to clean it up—or hire someone to do it for you. We'll explore more about energy and our environment in chapter 8.

Does social media, electronic devices, or any type of screen have too much of your attention? We have been inundated with devices and media over the last thirty years. Screens are everywhere, and messages never stop coming at us. Our ability to manage our devices and all of the information they provide us hasn't really caught up to the pace at which the information keeps coming. Believe it or not, "phone separation anxiety" is now an acknowledged phenomenon where people without their phones find it difficult to perform mental tasks without anxiety.

How about perfectionism? Incompletions (like this book was for me!)? The list of mental energy drains could go on for a long time. Consider your individual fears, pastimes, habits, obsessions, and more. You likely already know your trouble areas, but hopefully this section got you thinking so we can take out some of the withdrawals from our energy accounts and really start to make some deposits.

FOCUS

The number of things we can apply mental energy to is immeasurable. It's kind of strange that we could ever be bored, especially today. One key to great mental energy is to focus your mental energies on those things that you can influence. Dr. Stephen Covey describes is as "The Circle of Concern" and "The Circle of Influence." Imagine it like this: There is one large circle that contains all the matters of concern in your life. It includes thousands of things. Mental energy can be allocated to any of these things at any time— and can even take up a significant amount of time and energy.

Being focused asks us to consider which events, life issues, work issues, etc., falls into the Circle of Influence and which fall into the Circle of Concern. For example, you might be concerned that you may develop cancer or some other life threatening illness because it runs in your family. That's the Circle of Concern.

While you can't control the outcome, you can certainly influence it by eating right, exercising, and generally taking great care of yourself. That's the Circle of Influence. Rather than spending our mental energy focusing on whatever comes to mind, we choose to focus our energies on those things that we can do something about.

There may be significant and serious things that fall into that larger circle of concern that we simply still have no influence over. In other words, we can't do everything. Go ahead, say it to yourself: "I can't do everything!" **A person who protects their mental energy learns to discern between what they do and do not have influence over.**

When we focus our mental energy into our circle of influence, we can accomplish great things. Learn to set goals in the areas you have control over in your life. Go for wins, even the easy ones, and allow them to motivate you on to even greater goals. Your goals should be big enough to be significant, but small enough to accomplish within a reasonably short amount of time (losing forty kilograms over the next year is too much over too long to stay motivated). You should be able to accomplish your goals with reasonable effort (making an extra $5,000 next month may be possible, but at what expense?), and they should not always be out of desperation. Make some goals just for fun, and feel the satisfaction of winning. Make goals with your family or significant other. And make some goals that will benefit other people as well as yourself.

The great news is that when we focus on the areas that we can impact, the Circle of Influence expands and begins to overtake the Circle of Concern. Over time, you begin to develop and expand the areas of life that are important to you while selectively eliminating the outside issues and stressors in the Circle of Concern. This puts you in the driver's seat and increases the feeling of control, lessens the level of stress, and increases your mental energy.

REST

My favorite expression on rest is to "create white space." What does that mean? You know all those scribbles and blocked off areas in your calendar? Make some of it disappear. No plans, nothing to produce or accomplish, just make it white. Where can this happen in your daily routine? How about your week, month, or year? Doing nothing is rest and recovery time. It is time to appreciate all that you have done, and to reenergize yourself for all there is to be done. It is time to reward yourself. But it is so much more than just reward—it is necessary.

Our society values production over rest. So don't be alarmed when others are not supportive of your white space. You don't have to feel as though you deserve it before you take it. That's just part of being human, and it just happens to make us more productive. A recent study has shown that those who work in cycles of fifty-two minutes with seventeen minute breaks are more productive than those who put in even more hours.[7]

Resting is not nothingness. It is an intentional opportunity to recharge. It can also be an incredible time for creative flashes and ideas. Many of the world's best minds took time out to do nothing but think. One of my favorite current thought leaders is Robin Sharma, author of *The Monk Who Sold His Ferrari* and *The Leader Who Had No Titile*, among others. He says that he gets all of his best creative ideas for projects, workshops, and books when he's skiing. I know personally that the idea for this book came to me when I was laying in the sun on a beach in St. Lucia! Again, resting is not nothingness, and it is anything but nonproductive. But you don't have to be on a ski slope or beach. If you're resting through your day, then take time to stretch, rehydrate, eat a healthy snack, take a walk, or encourage someone. Weekly rests may include a lengthy nap, doing a puzzle, playing with the kids, taking a sight-seeing drive, or going out to dinner. I plan my yearly white space to be with family and intentionally assess the time since my previous lengthy break. I use that time to consider what I projects I wish to accomplish in my near future. The rest gives me clarity so I can be more intentional and effective over the coming months.

---

[7]Gifford, Julia. "The Rule of 52 and 17: It's Random, But It Ups Your Productivity." The Rule of 52 and 17: It's Random, But It Ups Your Productivity. 2014. Accessed June 30, 2016. https://www.themuse.com/advice/the-rule-of-52-and-17-its-random-but-it-ups-your-productivity.

Being mentally healthy goes beyond learning healthy bits of information (like reading this book) and staying aware of our current energy levels. It is a regular process of thinking about what you are thinking about, staying focused on our areas of influence and not outside of it, and practicing regular intentional rest. I hope this chapter has helped you to better understand the contributions our mental health has on our overall energy.

CHAPTER SUMMARY

Mental energy is the "brain power" that has incredible impact on our overall energy levels and well-being. The importance of our mental health cannot be understated. Throughout our days, we make mental attachments to various things. Sometimes these attachments become mindless compulsions, or as we like to call them, habits. Anytime we develop a dependence on substances to get us through our days, we are counterfeiting the mental energy our body is designed to provide and overdrawing our energy accounts. All of us get feelings of mild depression or the blues sometimes. Dr. Doug Sea offers a way of dealing with this. He explains that we have two perceptions about a situation— the way it "ought" to be, and the way it actually "is." When we get caught up in the illusion of what our mind thinks a situation "ought" to be, the result is feeling down, depressed, and generally low energy because we've created a state in our mind that we aren't enough or that we've failed. When we consciously choose to focus on what "is" and put effort into changing what "is," we can then eventually attain the "ought." Our minds and bodies are always interconnected. Our perception and thoughts can greatly affect the stress response in our body. Mental energy is inextricably tied to our thoughts, so we need to take responsibility for our thinking through awareness, focus, and mental rest time. One key to great mental energy is to focus your mental energies on those things that you can influence. Rather than spending our mental energy focusing on whatever comes to mind, we choose to focus our energies on those things that we can do something about. Being mentally healthy goes beyond learning healthy bits of information (like reading this book) and staying aware of our current energy levels. It is a regular process of being aware of what you are thinking about, staying focused on our areas of influence, and practicing regular intentional rest.

ACTION STEPS

- Try the rubber band method to help "snap" yourself out of negative thoughts and into a better state. Anytime you are overanxious or dwelling on something negative, snap a rubber band on your wrist to remind yourself to change your thinking.

- Try Shawn Achor's five steps over twenty-one days to limit your negativity and rewire your brain to be more positive. You'll be amazed at how your thinking and disposition changes!
- Look at your calendar and make some of it disappear. No plans, nothing to produce or accomplish, simply create some "white space." Do this in your daily routine as well as for your week, month, and year.

CHAPTER SIX

EMOTIONAL ENERGY

"Positive emotional energy is the key to health, happiness and well-being. The more positive you are, the better your life will be in every area."

– Brian Tracy

Emotional energy is the boost experienced when we connect with a great cause, receive affirmation, or empathize with a person. It's the inspirational stuff—the stuff movies are made about. It causes us to cheer for the underdog and helps the underdog rise to the occasion. It gives us a way to go beyond our limits and keeps us up late at night. Emotional energy can account for up to 70% of one's energy source, which translates into huge deposits to our overall energy account. But emotional energy can be fleeting. Just think about the last time someone asked you, "Do you want the good news or bad news first?" Because we can experience a broad range of emotions in a relatively short amount of time, emotional energy doesn't store well. But that's not to say it cannot be better understood and managed.

A healthy life will experience a broad spectrum of emotions, including love, joy, gratitude, and passion, as well as anger, fear, sadness, and frustration. While the good stuff fills us up, living persistently in the midst of negative emotions can result in significant energy withdrawals and health concerns, including lowered immunity, slower healing times, headaches, backaches, heart disease, cancer, and other degenerative conditions. Even the phrase "dying from a broken heart" is more than symbolic. Studies have shown that the likelihood of an elderly person having a heart attack or stroke doubles for thirty days after experiencing the death of a spouse. Other studies have observed decreased immune response during times of grief.

Our emotions have an incredible impact on our physical health as well. We observe this visually when something embarrassing is said about someone in their presence. Watch closely, and you'll see the blushing effect in their cheeks. What causes this? Firstly, recognize that they've attached a meaning to what was said that created the emotion of embarrassment. The same thing said to someone else may not embarrass them. The perception created the emotion that actually changes their physiology. Secondly, understand that with this embarrassing moment, a hormone called adrenalin is released, opening up the arteries in their cheeks, increasing blood flow and thus the red hue. This leaves us to wonder: if a simple embarrassment can leave such a distinguishable mark and drastically alter our physiology, what could other emotions do to our health in less obvious ways? That's a great question—and one that scientist Norman Cousins devoted his life to.

Cousins, among many other things, performed research on the biochemistry of human emotions at the School of Medicine at UCLA. He believed our emotions were a critical part of successfully fighting illness. On separate occasions, Cousins was diagnosed with heart disease and a form of arthritis. He treated each by taking massive doses of Vitamin C and teaching himself to laugh. Upon being told he had little chance of surviving the diagnosis of ankylosing spondylitis, he moved out of the hospital and checked into a hotel across the street. There, he received his vitamin C doses intravenously and laughed during episodes of the Marx Brothers shown on a projector film. He states, "I made the joyous discovery that ten minutes of genuine belly laughter had an anesthetic effect and would give me at least two hours of pain-free sleep. When the pain-killing effect of the laughter wore off, we would switch on the motion picture projector again and, not infrequently, it would lead to another pain-free interval." Dr. Cousins literally laughed his way back to health, eventually dying at the age of seventy-five, decades after receiving his grim diagnosis.

THE PHYSIOLOGY OF EMOTION

What we think and feel emotionally is inseparable from what physiologically occurs in our body. That is why it is so important to realize just how much control we have over our emotions. Emotions are nothing more than a meaning we attach to something. This means that when we change our meaning or response to a situation, we can limit the physiological changes or stress response. When we feel negative emotions and are feeling stressed, our body releases hormones that decrease our energy and suppress our healing abilities. When we feel positive emotions, we release a cascade of feel-good hormones that dramatically increases our energy levels and healing capabilities. This concept is now becoming well known in medical journals and has implications in all diseases. For example, a study done by Dr. Chris Peterson explored optimism and pessimism in men who had just had their first heart attack. A total of 122 men who had a heart attack were evaluated on their outlook, or degree of optimism or pessimism. Eight years after the initial evaluation, twenty-one of the twenty-five of the most pessimistic men were dead. Amazingly, nineteen of the twenty-five most optimistic men where alive. This means that only six optimistic men died while twenty-one of the pessimists died. Further, the mental outlook of these men served as a greater predictor of survival than any other more typical risk factor—more than artery blockage, cholesterol level, blood pressure, and even more than the actual damage done to the heart in the first heart attack. Other research in this area indicates that those individuals with a more optimistic outlook who underwent arterial bypass surgery recovered much quicker with less complications from the surgery.[8]

Another study exploring the effects of emotional state and physiological health was published in *Cancer Research* called "The Sympathetic Nervous System Induces a Metastatic Switch in Primary Breast Cancer." This essentially means that the "fight or flight" system that we talked about earlier causes an increase in metastasis, or spreading of the cancer from the breast to other tissues. The authors found that an increase in stress and its effects on the neuroendocrine system "induced a 30-fold increase in metastasis to distant tissues including lymph nodes and lung."[9]

We all have likely witnessed people who have either overcome incredible odds or succumbed to a health challenge though the conscious choice of their thoughts and emotions. Kris Carr is an incredible example of what is possible through taking control of your emotions, dropping the stress, and as a result, living and taking responsibility for an incredible life. Carr was diagnosed with an incurable form of stage 4 cancer. With that diagnosis, Kris did not opt to just go home and get her things in order; instead, she chose

---

[8]C. Peterson et al., Learned Helplessness: A Theory for the Age of Personal Control (New York; Oxford University Press, 1993.)

[9]E. Sloan et al., Cancer Research September 15, 2010 70; 7042.

live her life full out and to start participating in her well-being. She made an incredible film called *Crazy, Sexy Cancer*, has written several books, and runs a mission-driven business that helps others with cancer and inspires possibilities in all people. Amazingly, she just surpassed her tenth year after her diagnosis, and while there is still no cure for her condition, her tumors have shrunk, and she says that she is living a more connected and magical life than before her diagnosis. Emotional energy is powerful, and the best part is, like Kris Carr, you have the power and ability to harness and control it.

How? Be aware and know that there is a stimulus and a little gap before the response. We don't have to be victims to our emotions (or our health). This puts us back in the driver's seat to take control and choose a different response. This in turn makes big changes in our health and physiology. But it takes a lot of practice and is a constant work in progress. That is where emotional intelligence comes in.

EMOTIONAL INTELLIGENCE

"Between stimulus and response there is a space. In that space is our power to choose our response. In our response lies our growth and our freedom."

– Dr. Viktor E. Frankl

Emotional intelligence is about being proactive and taking owner-ship for one's own emotions. Those who lack it live like they are riding a roller-coaster, only able to react to the previous twist or turn in their emotions. Because of this, their personal decisions are often shortsighted and emotionally driven. Having emotional intel-ligence certainly doesn't remove the adventure of life, but where lacking it feels like being a passive roll-roller coaster rider, having it is like being the driver of an off-road vehicle on a great adventure. We aren't sure what's coming, but we have some tools to help us navigate and respond. The good news is that this is a skill you can learn and continue to work on. Having emotional intelligence is about awareness, personal ownership, and living in community.

Awareness

Once again, we recognize that moving forward is about aware-ness—knowing where we start so we can move forward. Once we experience awareness, we can't unknow it. Equally, it is some-thing we need to practice on an ongoing basis throughout the day. Emotional awareness is about discriminating between feelings and labeling them appropriately. I have found myself in situations where it was easy to react in anger, and I didn't even recognize that it was anger I was experiencing. In the moment I thought I was being perfectly rational. Did you know that studies[10] have shown us that when we are angry, our IQ plummets? Recognizing when we are acting in anger can save us from some costly decisions!

Mindfulness is a great place to start when we are learning to become aware of and recognize our emotions. There is a wealth of information out there on mindfulness, and it is well worth taking some trainings or familiarizing yourself with the concept in books or articles. Basically, being mindful means being aware of our thoughts, feelings, sensations, and physical environment on a moment-by-moment basis. It is a really simple concept and requires ongoing practice. It asks that we pause, observe, and accept what is going on in and around us. It's the foundation for reducing stress, discovering our passions, and taking control during the gap between stimulus and response. It's the first step to recognizing how we feel.

I liken mindfulness to the first step of a technique I learned from my mentor Dr. Frank Sovinsky called the "Triple A Bond" technique. The first step is to acknowledge. When working with patients, this means I acknowledge what I hear them say regarding their pain or condition. I don't judge or challenge it. I simply accept it for what it is. We can also apply this to ourselves. When we are being mindful, we acknowledge what we feel, think, see, hear, or taste.

---

[10]Nadler, Relly, Psy.D., M.C.C. "Where Did My IQ Points Go?" Psychology Today. April 29, 2011. Accessed June 30, 2016. https://www.psychologytoday.com/blog/leading-emotional-intelligence/201104/where-did-my-iq-points-go.

Once we are able to recognize what we experience, we can take the second step of evaluating what caused it.

Management

Having the ability to stop and recognize what we are feeling is necessary personal emotional management. Now that we know *what* we are experiencing, management is asking *how* are we going to respond. In other words, let's invite our mental cognition into the situation before our emotional feelings run amuck!

This is similar to the second step in Dr. Sovinsky's technique: ask. In the scenario with my patient, I ask a question to better understand what I just acknowledged. It might be to clarify, seek further information, or explore a potential solution. Again, we can apply this to our emotional intelligence with ourselves. Here, we get curious and ask a question that might point us to a cause or a possible response.

Living in Community

The previous two processes are necessary so that we can best live in community with others. Living in community means that we not only recognize and appreciate our own feelings but also respect and protect the feelings of others. We are able to show empathy, celebrate alongside others, and contribute to their needs. One way we do this is when we apply the third step of the "Triple A Bond" technique: answer. With my patients, this is when I offer my support, encouragement, or advice. With myself, this is where I choose a response based on my recognition and appreciation of my feelings.

Life can sometimes become a process of moving through mundane days, and it can cause us to forget that we are emotional beings. Emotional intelligence is the ability to recognize our emotions, embrace both the highs and lows of life, and see how our emotions contribute to who we are. If you would like to read further about understanding and controlling your emotions, check out Daniel Goleman's book *Emotional Intelligence*.

KNOWING YOUR VALUES

Knowing our values is a personal matter. A host of factors, including genetics, culture, and life experiences, are involved in making each of us wonderfully unique. As we gain greater self-awareness, we learn to better appreciate others and live a life "leaning into" the things that we value and gain fulfillment from.

There are several things you can do to better understand your values. The most basic is to simply observe yourself. How do you spend your time and money? Why? When do you feel the most fulfilled? What things do you surround yourself with? Who are the people you choose to be with? Where are you when you feel your best? As a fair warning: when you answer these questions, you may not like the values that are revealed. But give yourself some grace and know that an honest assessment is necessary to move forward.

As I look around my office, I see lots of books on health, business, and finances. Learning is part of my personality, and I greatly value the topics of those books. My wife places great value in aesthetics. She loves to make things look great, and it gives her great energy to create order, improve how a room looks, or wear clothes that look great on her. Together we benefit from each other's values.

Understanding your personality is another great way to gain insight into your values. There are many legitimate personality tests and behavioral assessments that are available online today. I like to recommend the DISC and values assessment.

The value of learning about yourself through such tools is twofold. First, you will learn some things about yourself and what makes you "tick." In fact, the results should help you go beyond knowing what drives you and what annoys you to understanding why. It also allows us to understand and appreciate how each of us is different. What is an emotional energizer for me may be a significant downer for someone else, and vice versa. When we grasp this, we better learn how to protect our own values and still appreciate the values of others.

We all like to be stroked, and there are some of us who have fallen into the trap of doing almost anything to gain approval from others. They live according to the expectations of other people and forfeit their own values. The result can be losing self-identity, and sometimes self-respect. Over time, these poor souls find themselves emotionally lifeless. Compliments and approval are rewarding, but there is nothing more rewarding than receiving them for being true to ourselves. Take the time to get to know yourself well; it's an investment worth taking. And doing so will give you what is needed to take the final step—making some changes.

MAKE SOME CHANGES

Making changes in your life can be incredibly difficult (especially if you've been living to please others) because you will need to say "no" to some of those emotional-energy-sucking activities or people. It's a task worth doing. If you want to say "yes" to the great things in your life, you're going to have to say "no" to even some of the good things.[11] Don't go about this step in a rush, and be sure to give consideration to your values and the values of your family members as well.

---

[11]Check out *Boundaries: When to Say Yes, How to Say No to Take Control of Your Life* by Henry Cloud and John Townsend.

Consider sitting down with your family, a large sheet of white paper, and some markers. Ask some questions about what each person values, and start making plans to fill each other's energy account emotionally. Talk about the music they love, when they feel their best, what family traditions they love the best, what excites them about each holiday, and so much more. Not only will this provide you direction for a great future but it will also fill you with great memories and appreciation for your past!

As I have encouraged several times already in this book, consider taking time to journal. Simply carry something with you for a week that you are able to jot down ideas, thoughts, frustrations, and highlights into. Was there a great song that came on the radio that lifted you up? Did you try something new this morning that started your day off better? Was there an encounter with a person that energized you? And what were the low points as well? This will allow you to be more intentional about making emotional energy deposits and protect yourself from unnecessary withdrawals.

Norman Cousins had suspected all along what so many in the health field are now coming to accept: our well-being is so much more than our physical bodies. To be whole and live a life full of energy, we need to develop awareness and adopt a healthy lifestyle physically, mentally, emotionally, and in the next chapter, we will discuss our spiritual lives.

CHAPTER SUMMARY

Emotions are a huge source of energy that can have huge consequences on our lives, health, and other energy sources based on
whether or not we experience positive or negative emotions. What
we think and feel emotionally is inseparable from what physiologically occurs in our body. That is why it is so important to realize
just how much control we have over our emotions. We have all
likely witnessed people who have either overcome incredible odds
or succumbed to health challenges though their conscious choice
of thoughts and emotions. Emotional energy is powerful, and the
best part is we have the power and ability to harness and control it.
One way is by practicing emotional intelligence. Emotional intelligence is about being proactive and taking ownership for your own
emotions. Having emotional intelligence is about awareness, personal ownership, and living in community. It is the ability to recognize our emotions, embrace both the highs and lows of life, and
see how our emotions contribute to who we are. As we gain greater
self-awareness, we learn to better appreciate others and live a life
"leaning into" the things that we value and find fulfillment from.
Take the time to get to know yourself well; it's an investment worth
taking. And doing so will give you what is needed to take the final
step—making some changes. To be whole and live a life full of
energy, we need to develop awareness and adopt a healthy lifestyle

physically, mentally, and emotionally, and in the next chapter, we will discuss our spiritual lives.

ACTION STEPS

- Better understand your values. Do this by observing yourself, understanding your personality, and/or sitting down with your family.
- Learn more about mindfulness training by attending classes or reading books and articles.
- Take time to journal. Simply carry something with you for a week that you are able to jot down ideas, thoughts, frustrations, and highlights into. This will allow you to be more intentional about making emotional energy deposits and protect yourself from unnecessary withdrawals.

CHAPTER SEVEN

SPIRITUAL ENERGY

"What God intended for you goes far beyond anything you can imagine."

– Oprah Winfrey

Spiritual energy is deeply personal and remarkably powerful. It is also rather ambiguous and often misunderstood. There are many ways to handle this type of energy, and the topic certainly deserves more than just a chapter. My desire is to help you gain a little understanding of how spiritual energy may or may not be contributing to your life and energy, and give you a few pointers on how you can make it a highly significant part of your overall well-being.

On one hand, we can discuss spiritual energy as a matter of quantum physics—science that is incredibly theoretical and full of potential yet to be unlocked. On the other, we could discuss it in the therapeutic sense—highly preferential and relative, it becomes whatever makes us feel good. For the sake of keeping this simple and practical, I am going to discuss spiritual energy as that immaterial part of ourselves that binds all the rest of us together and makes up who we truly are. It's the "me" that goes beyond what others see and know about me.

In my opinion, spiritual energy is the most powerful of all the energies. It is the catalyst for motivation and hope. It often defies explanation and leaves us in awe when we experience it or see it in others. This is the stuff movies are made of. Characters with unflinching resilience, steadfast conviction, and remarkable ability who have tapped into something immeasurable that I label spiritual energy. Consider the likes of Rosa Parks, Winston Churchill, and Martin Luther King. Think of Terry Fox and Rick Hanson and their life missions. Think of Oprah Winfrey. Each were endowed with incredible spiritual energy that gave them the courage and resolve to become larger than life. They were each INSPIRING!

This is one of my favorite words—inspiring. When we allow our spiritual selves to come alive, we begin to live an inspiring life! Inspiration is that stuff we see in superheroes and people who just seem to be larger than life. Being an inspiration is being of great mind and heart, lofty, generous, and not petty. Inspiring people are not easily offended. They encounter danger and trouble with tranquility and firmness. They elevate their souls and minds to consider beyond the present crises, and yet are empathetic and generous toward the concerns of those around them. Wow! I believe we all have that spiritual ability.

Do you now see how your spiritual wellness becomes the multiplier of all other sources of energy? Our spiritual selves provide a huge part of our identity by giving us perspective, empowering us beyond accepted limitations, and giving us clarity and purpose. Whereas the previous three sources of energy help keep your boat afloat and plug the leaks, your spiritual self determines just what sort of boat you are aboard. Which would you prefer to navigate through life with: a dingy or an ocean liner?

Spiritual energy has an incredible impact on our health, and its deficits may be the most difficult to detect until crisis strikes. And because it is so neglected and generally misunderstood, it sometimes goes too long without being identified. The telltale signs of those with a spiritual health deficit are that they do not value others or themselves, and they live life in a hectic rush, are rarely grateful, use people and love things, and live thinking that they are in control of their own lives. Often, they have the delusion that they bring about all that is good in their life, and that someone else is responsible for all the bad. And all of this brings an incredible amount of anxiety along with it. Does this ring true for you? I know I've experienced all of those signs at one time or another. In fact, somedays I still do.

The underlying cause of this sort of life is the feeling and belief that we are not enough. It can bring with it the unsettled, uneasy feeling that something is missing—somehow our life is coming up short of what it ought to be. So we either franticly pursue or just give up. Most of the time, we do a little of both, neither of which brings us a sense of contentment. It is worth paying close attention to the messages being sent to us by marketers. Almost all marketing campaigns are designed to make you feel insufficient.

They send the message, "You are not enough without my product." And it works.

I believe each of us is intentionally created. But without this conviction, we can live our lives inauthentically. Not in a deceitful way, but in the sense of not being true to ourselves. When we are stuck in this place, we spend our time and energies accommodating those around us and only play a persona or part of who we really are. You don't need to live this way.

The first step to overcome this kind of living is to recognize that we are not merely physical and chemical beings, but rather we are divine and spiritual beings with purpose presently living in a body. Dr. Wayne Dyer says that we are not human beings having a spiritual experience; we are spiritual beings having a human experience. We are so much more than we realize! I understand this is where some of you may be tempted to get off the Rest Ethic Express, but hang with me for just a few more pages! I am convinced that the lack of acknowledgement of our spiritual selves is what is keeping so many of us from living a full life. While I have my own religious convictions that contribute greatly to my spiritual well-being, this is not an attempt to proselytize. I encourage you to intentionally search within and beyond yourself for what it means to be a spiritual being.

Tapping into our spiritual energy source provides us with a sense of purpose and perspective like nothing else. When we see that we are not in control of all things and learn how to handle the ups and downs of life, recognizing that we are sometimes a very thin, but immensely important, part of the grand narrative that is life around us, we live more intentionally. We set ourselves free from those things that we cannot change and put our energies into the places where we are uniquely equipped to make a difference. In short, we live inspired! Does this mean that we become so disconnected with life that we are no darn earthly good? By all means, no! We will experience highs and lows, but with a better eye toward the future and with great hope for what is yet to come.

Living an inspired life is more than a choice. It must be cultivated and it must also experience detachment from the ways of the rest of society. Here are some great first steps to unlock that inspirational you!

BE SILENT

Take the time to be still. You are more than a reactionary being to all the stuff that happens around you. Just *be* for a little while each day. In this time, you may choose to meditate or to pray. But most of all, I encourage you to listen. Listening is not fretting about your day; it's just being and hearing what your body has to say, or what your god has to say.

My morning quiet time, sometimes before I even get out of bed, is one of the best parts of my day. I cherish the time that I can spend with God and give him my cares. It was Saint Augustine that shared, "Pray like it all depends on God and work like it all depends on you." I find a lot of comfort in that statement, and it allows me to move forward in my day focused on my own Circle of Influence.

FEED

Spend some time feeding your soul through spirtual writings. It may be your Bible, a favorite devotional, proverbs, teachings from a pastor, or the written works of ancient sages. Go beyond feeding your soul with cute saying found on Facebook or blogs and find some real gems. If you have a holy book, such as a Bible, invest in it. Research things like translations and consider carefully the one you want to purchase. Consider things like size, font, and study notes. Make it something special that you will want to come back to. Find one with a beautiful cover and give it the value and attention it deserves. I know, you can just download a free one on your phone, but statistics have shown that they are rarely read.

ACCEPT AND LET GO

Inspiring people are those who accept and let go. Do what you can, and always do what only you can, and let the rest go to God. When you are offended—and we can experience horrible offenses—know that it need not define you or write the rest of your story.

One of the joys I have in my line of work is working with people who are experiencing tragic illnesses or injuries, sometimes terminal, and seeing how they are able to live each day with incredible peace. They are my heroes! They have learned the art of accepting and letting go. Let me be clear, they have not quit. But they have accepted their current circumstances and are secure that they are doing all that is reasonable to positively influence their future outcome. They know that ultimately their life is out of their control and they choose to live each day for everything it has to offer. They don't miss the opportunity to bless others by focusing on themselves.

STOP

You may have heard of the word "sabbath" as a concept present in various religions. The word sabbath simply means "stop." Ask yourself, "When is the last time I really just stopped?" I mean really just stopped all that was going on: no inputs, no entertainment, nothing. You have been designed to stop every once in a while. When you look to the Bible and other religious teachings, you learn that even God took a day off! In my opinion, this is a great reminder that we are not meant to be "always on."

I have a friend who is of Jewish faith. He shared with me that on the Sabbath, they have a tradition of putting a wine glass on a plate and then filling the glass until it overflows onto the plate beneath.

This serves as a powerful reminder to the people of his faith that we must be still enough to be filled up to the point of overflowing if we wish to bless others. We cannot give what we do not have! When you learn to say "no" and stop more often, you will undoubtedly have those who will not understand and ask you for your time. And sometimes the best way to serve them is to make sure you are filled up first so you have something to give.

DO COMMUNITY

Don't go through life alone. I'm a firm believer that we are meant to do life together. In healthy community, you not only benefit but also contribute to the lives of others. You will find that you can have a life full of unofficial mentors whom you learn from when you do community together. It takes time, it takes effort, it takes breaking the habit of driving into your garage each afternoon not to be seen again until the following day at work. But it is well worth it!

BE GRATEFUL

I began the practice of having a gratitude journal some time back. If I don't take time to write three things I am grateful for each morning, then I at least try to bring to mind three things as I drive to work. It is amazing what "counting your blessings" does to your well-being. It is a constant reminder to me that I did not get here alone and it keeps me humble. Recent research suggests that feelings of thankfulness helps people cope with life problems and stress. Elevate your spiritual energy by taking time to be grateful!

I am convinced that there is a spiritual giant inside of each of us. We each have the capacity to rise above and become inspirational—to live confidently and be at peace with ourselves. Spiritual energy is about profound presence and purpose, and it is well within reach of each of us. My hope is that I am able to have even the slightest influence in helping you awaken your spirit to help you be all that you can be.

Spiritual energy is all encompassing and impacts all three other sources of energy we've talked about. High spiritual energy connects us to our highest self and helps us live out our potential. Our emotional energy can fuel us or drain us on that journey. Positive emotions can fill our reserves, while negative emotions, while still purposeful, can empty our emotional fuel tanks. High mental energy can give us the flexibility and adaptability along our path. When overextended, overworked, or overchallenged, our mental energy can falter and leave us rigid, inflexible, and frustrated. Our physical energy is our foundation, and serves to help us carry out and live out our lives. High physical energy can be the driver for other energies and carry us along our life journey.

Now that we have learned about the four sources of energy in our lives, we are going to get very practical. Join me as we learn about the rested lifestyle.

CHAPTER SUMMARY

Spiritual energy is deeply personal and remarkably powerful. It is also rather ambiguous and often misunderstood. For the sake of keeping this simple and practical, I define spiritual energy as that immaterial part of ourselves that binds all the rest of us together and makes up who we truly are. It's the "me" that goes beyond what others see and know about me. In my opinion, spiritual energy is the most powerful of all energies. It is the catalyst for motivation and hope. Our spiritual selves provide a huge part of our identity by giving us perspective, empowering us beyond accepted limitations, and giving us clarity and purpose. Spiritual energy has an incredible impact on our health, and its deficits may be the most difficult to detect until crisis strikes. The telltale signs of those with a spiritual health deficit are that they do not value others or themselves, they live life in a hectic rush, and they are rarely grateful, use people and love things, and live thinking that they are in control of their life. The first step to overcoming this kind of living is to recognize that we are not merely physical and chemical beings, but rather we are divine and spiritual beings with purpose presently living in a bodily condition. Tapping into our spiritual energy source provides us with a sense of purpose and perspective like nothing else. When we see that we are not in control of all things and learn how to handle the ups and downs of life, recognizing that we are sometimes a very thin, but immensely important, part of the grand narrative that is life around us, we live more intentionally. We do this by getting silent, feeding our souls, learning to accept and let go, learning to stop and say "no," finding a community, and practicing gratitude. Spiritual energy is about profound presence and purpose, and it is well within reach of each of us.

ACTION STEPS

- Take the time to be still and silent a few minutes each day.
- Find a group or community of unofficial mentors whom you can learn from.
- Take time to write down three things you are grateful for each morning or night.

CHAPTER EIGHT

LIFESTYLE—SPACES AND RELATIONSHIPS

"Sometimes the biggest gain in productive energy will come from cleaning the cobwebs, dealing with old business, and clearing the desks—cutting loose debris that is impeding forward motion."

– David Allen

Now that we have covered the four forms in which we can deposit energy and by which we have energy withdrawals, let's dive into some practical matters. This chapter is about our day-to-day living and how our environments and relationships can contribute to our ability to focus on the task of rest.

The spaces we inhabit have a great deal of impact on our ability to function. Notre Dame football is so convinced of this that, in contrast to the ornate, masculine locker room they provide their own team, the visiting locker room is pink—complete with pink urinals and all.

"In the 1950s prizewinning biologist and doctor Jonas Salk was working on a cure for polio in a dark basement laboratory in

Pittsburgh. Progress was slow, so to clear his head, Salk traveled to Assisi, Italy, where he spent time in a 13th-century monastery, ambling amid its columns and cloistered courtyards. Suddenly, Salk found himself awash in new insights, including the one that would lead to his successful polio vaccine. Salk was convinced he had drawn his inspiration from the contemplative setting. He came to believe so strongly in architecture's ability to influence the mind that he teamed up with renowned architect Louis Kahn to build the Salk Institute in La Jolla, Calif., as a scientific facility that would stimulate breakthroughs and encourage creativity."[12]

While the notion that our environments have influence on the way we function has long been assumed, science is gaining ground to find empirical data to that effect as well. Our environments are extensions of ourselves, and what is in our environment will contribute to our energy by providing focus and the right frame of mind. For example, I have found a library study room away from distraction that I am able to sign out in order to write this chapter. I turn out the lights in the room, put on headphones, and listen to music that allows me to best concentrate. The environment makes the difference. Conversely, our environment can be an energy detractor if it has distractions or leaves us feeling unsettled.

---

[12]Anthes, Emily. Scientific American. "How Room Designs Affect Your Work and Mood." April/May/June 2009.

Long-term exposure to environments even has the ability to influence our beliefs and values.

THREE MEASURES

As we discuss the different environments we move in and out of each day, I'd like to consider whether they are clean and decluttered, whether they are fully functional, and how they pass a sensory check.

Clean and Declutter

First, clutter and uncleanliness bombard our mind with unnecessary stimuli. When we attempt to focus on the task at hand, or on rest, our mind has too many other things that are taking up its periphery, preventing it from giving the task at hand all the attention it deserves. Not to mention, clutter sort of wears on us and provides anxiety as we wonder, "just when will I ever be able to attend to that mess?" And finally, it is a time waster. How many times should you have to look for your keys underneath piles of paper or laundry?

The great news is that clutter and uncleanliness are among the easiest energy wasters to address. There is tons of information available about decluttering and simplifying our lives, and there are stores that have made a business out of tasteful organization. While I am not able to give an exhaustive lesson on decluttering (and if you saw my car, you would think me unqualified to speak on the subject), here are a couple of tips I would like to share. First, if you don't use it, throw it. Too often, clutter occurs because we suffer from the "maybe someday" syndrome. If you cannot think of a specific need for an item in the near future or a time you used it in the recent past, then it is probably not necessary. And second, touch it once. That is, when you receive items like mail, make an attempt to only have to touch it once. Each piece either gets thrown (most), responded to (sometimes), or filed (rarely). If the information on the piece of mail can be accessed another way (i.e., the Internet), then it is unnecessary to keep it. Preserving our energy and protecting our creativity is all about simplifying. There is much to learn on the subject, and I hope you are able to see how it applies to the areas of your life as we move forward.

Function

As I prepared for this chapter, I was reminded that I had a cabinet door in my house that I must have opened thirty times already, each time noticing that it does not swing correctly. So I stopped, got my screwdriver, and fixed it. The sense of reward was ridiculously disproportionate to the amount of work it took to fix it. Each time

I used that cabinet, I would experience a sense of frustration that was simply unnecessary. If you have undone projects growing around you, take the time to address a few. I hope you get just as much satisfaction out of it as I did with my cabinet door.

Sensory Check

Our bodies respond to sensory stimulation in a multitude of ways. We are still learning about how we react to certain smells, sounds, colors, and touches. There are certain smells that can stop you in your tracks—freshly baked bread or hot-from-the-oven chocolate chip cookies. Or there are other smells, like harsh chemicals or some perfumes (that are sprayed on by the gallon), that can make you feel physically ill. And she has others she puts on that, well ... I like them.

Our senses are always at work, and preserving our energy and maintaining focus is about avoiding the agitation that comes when we are picking up on things that are unnecessary. When we do the sensory check in different environments, we are asking ourselves to experience spaces as though we are coming into them for the first time. We have to ask ourselves, what am I hearing now that I have just accepted as normal? What smells need to be eliminated, and are there others to be introduced? Do the lights and colors in this room bring me calm? Energize me? Or do they kill my mood? Most sensory improvements require minimal effort and resources, but they have to be recognized.

Now, let's apply these investigative tools to the spaces we typically spend our days in.

ENVIRONMENTS

In a typical day, each of us moves through four environments that we have control over: our home, sleep environment, transportation, and workspace. None of these is an isolated space. Each one of them contributes to how you perform in the others—especially our sleep environment, so I am devoting an entire chapter to that topic next.

Home

Your home is your sanctuary and the place you should feel most fulfilled and rested. It should also be a safe place, free of anxiety and unnecessary disturbances. It's the place that prepares you to go out and give the world your best, and it is the place that you establish to nurture and raise your children. As T.S. Eliot states, "Home is where one starts from." And it is true. Every day, your home is your catalyst, and it is your respite at the end of your day as well. Thoughts of home should always bring a smile to your face.

Take a mental scan of your home. Is your energy safe there? Does it need to be cleaned or decluttered? Is stuff stored nicely out of sight? How much time do you have to spend in frustration searching for the remote or your checkbook? Are there dirty corners or bathrooms that get ignored? I just remembered that I have some boxes from last year's move that are a constant reminder of unfinished business. They nag at me, and you and I both know it will only do me good to take some time to get them off my to-do list.

How is your home, functionally? I once lived in a home where the garage door did not close whenever the weather dropped below a certain temperature. I spent two winters having to jump out of our vehicles, hold the button down to override the sensor, and wait in the cold for the door to close before I could jump back in the car. Did I mention it only did this in the cold? Just imagine how I felt after performing the thirty-dollar, twenty-minute fix just before selling the house. I almost didn't want to move out. It was not a major thing, but that energy and time waster introduced unnecessary agitation into our lives every cold day of the year. How are your faucets? Appliances? Door hinges and latches? Don't let this stuff add up. Instead, take advantage of YouTube "how-to" videos and feel the satisfaction of completing the job and living with a little less stress in your life.

Give your home a sensory check. Are you really happy with the decor? Smell? Lighting? You can find many inexpensive decorating ideas online and change things up a little bit. My wife and I lived in a home that had a pink kitchen. And, like the garage door, we fixed it before we moved out. We had no idea just how much of an irritant the pink was until we sold the kitchen to someone else.

In the next week, try creating a private little space of peace for yourself. It could just be a corner with a chair and some natural lighting. I have a little personal space that has my guitar and some of my favorite books in it. Maybe you'll need to create some boundaries in that space, like choosing to not answer the phone, e-mails, or texts while in that space. Make it yours and make it something that revives you.

Sleep Space

We are devoting the entire next chapter to sleep, so I won't give everything away now. The importance of our sleep to our health cannot be overstated. So go through the check. Is your sleep space clean and decluttered so that you don't have nightmares before you drift off to dreamland? Can you fall asleep anxiety free? Is your stuff stored out of sight rather than openly on shelves? Are your clothes put away nicely?

It is so easy for the bedroom to become the store-all space in a house because it is the one place that guests are not going to see. But I say it is more important that you live in a clutter-free home than it is for the visitors who stop by for a visit. Protect your sleep space by keeping it free from clutter.

Keep everything functioning in that space—replace the light-bulbs, fix the ceiling fan, and do something about the break in the blinds. The sense of accomplishment alone will help you fall fast asleep!

And, finally, what do you sense in your bedroom? Do you like it? Does your room smell like something restful, or do you smell that dirty sock? Do you have ambient or candle lighting available to you, or only overhead lighting? Is the color of the room tranquil or loud? Is the room quiet enough to sleep well? What sounds would you like to introduce?

As a chiropractor, I have been asked many times what I recommend in a mattress (usually by a husband who wants me to say bricks and a wife who is hoping I say clouds). The truth is, it varies. Different things work for different people. Not too long ago, my wife picked up some new bedding, and I couldn't believe the difference it made. It kind of gets me excited about heading to bed. I want you to experience the same. Go make an investment in some pillows, bedding, and maybe even a new mattress. Some stores will allow you to try them out to see if they work for you. You will thank me the next morning.

Transportation

Some commutes are rather lengthy, and I know some of you may be in a vehicle up to three hours a day. Redeem the drive and make it more than just a necessity to get where you are going by putting it to our three measures. Remember, the time spent in transportation is your transition time when you prepare for what is next. It is key that you arrive ready to go, not recovering from the lousy commute.

Is your vehicle cluttered or dirty? Do you like the look of it, or do you park way in the back and hope nobody notices? How much stuff is stacked up on the floor boards? Can you write your name in the dust on the dash? After I clean up my car, it is as if someone has just gifted me with a new one. I sometimes forget just how good my car feels when the mess is gone. That trash in the periphery of your consciousness while you are driving just doesn't deserve your attention. Allow no more free rides for that bag of Goodwill donations that has been riding in your backseat for weeks. Let's clean those windows so you don't have to look through greasy fingerprints anymore. Come on, you know you can love that car again.

Unless it is not functioning well. Then this will get a little more involved. A poorly running vehicle causes anxiety. Consider if it is worth fixing and know that, if you have the funds, putting it off won't make it any better. Cars don't heal.

Does the car pass the sense check? Does it smell okay, or is there something rotting under the seat? Do you like the way it looks? Does the seat still feel comfortable? Some might call these things trivial, but I say if you have the ability to do something about them and they help you feel energized in your day, then they are necessary.

So, what do you think? I'm not proposing financial irresponsibility when I say that the dependability and likability of your vehicle needs to be addressed if there is a problem, but if it needs to be fixed or replaced, let's get it done. Or, at least start with an oil change, car wash, and new air freshener!

Work Environment

Most of us have *some* level of control of our work environment. What things do you have authority over in your workspace and what changes need to be made? Even if you don't have a personal space in your work environment, you and your coworkers could benefit from a bit of decluttering and cleaning. How is your desk? Do you like to sit at it, or is it just miserably stressful? When you leave at the end of the day, consider what you want to see the next morning when you arrive. How do you want to welcome yourself back to work? If your plant is giving up on the space, it's a pretty good sign that it isn't good for you, either.

The functionality of all the equipment at your workplace may be out of your control. But if you have a broken stapler, toss it! Take a few minutes to see if you can fix that chair. If you're a manager and you know your employees have been walking around that broken copier—move it or fix it. Working with broken stuff sends a devaluing message to the worker. Ditch the junk and move forward—you've been working around it all anyhow.

For some of us, it is very easy to make sensory changes in our workplace. Just think, what would be best for you to hear, smell, feel, and see. If you are working in a meat-packing plant, you don't get to choose the smell or the view. But I bet if you get creative enough, you can at least bring small improvements to your sensory experiences wherever you work.

Take some assessments over the next few days at work and make a couple of changes. Do something that is going to make your work experience a little more enjoyable. Because I don't know where you work, I have no idea what this could look like, but I'd love to hear some of your creative stories.

YOUR WARDROBE

What you wear is not really an environment, but it does have a real impact on how you feel, others people's impression of you, and what you think of yourself. A good friend, colleague, and mentor of mine

Dr. Cecile Thackeray developed a program called Corestyle™. Not only is she a gifted chiropractor, but she has an amazing aesthetic side to her personality and helps professionals develop a wardrobe that matches their personality. It brings out their authenticity and really resonates with who they are. I've gone through this process and have been amazed at my own transformation, as well as the radical changes in others.

What about you? Do your clothes fit you well, are they current, do they match your behavior style? Or do you still wear your lime-green leisure suit from the '70s? Maybe MC Hammer pants to the gym? (Gosh I hope not!—sorry, Hammer) Is your work attire current and appropriate for your age and your profession and just a great fit for you? This is an area I encourage you to invest in. Buy the best clothes that you can afford and that make you look great and feel good. It isn't vanity; it's valuing yourself. Consider it your wrapping paper!

Nothing I shared in this chapter is revolutionary, but I hope it serves as the motivation to do the simple things in your life to help you move forward with focused energy, not distracted by the little annoyances that can add up around you. When you invest so much in depositing energy into your life physically, mentally, emotionally, and spiritually, you need to protect those investments from little energy suckers that get into your daily routines. We are going to discuss sleep in the next chapter, but don't get too far ahead before you take care of some of the assignments above.

CHAPTER SUMMARY

This chapter is about our day-to-day living and how our environments and relationships can contribute to our ability to focus on a task or rest. The spaces we inhabit have a great deal of impact on our ability to function. Our environments are extensions of ourselves, and what is in our environment will either contribute to our energy by providing focus and the right frame of mind or drain it. There are four different environments we move in and out of each day, and it's important to consider whether they are clean and decluttered, whether they are fully functional, and how they pass a sensory check. The four environments that we have control over are: our home, sleep environment, transportation, and workspace. Our senses are always at work, and preserving our energy and maintaining focus is about avoiding the agitation that comes when we pick up on things that are unnecessary. When you invest so much in depositing energy into your life physically, mentally, emotionally, and spiritually, you need to protect those investments from little energy suckers that get into your daily routines.

ACTION STEPS

- Take an assessment of the amount of clutter you have in your home, sleep environment, car, and workspace. Pick one area to work on and make a few small changes to reduce the clutter and free up some mental and emotional energy.

- Take an assessment of the functionality of your four environments. If you have undone projects growing around you, take the time to address a few and feel the deep satisfaction that brings.

- Do a sensory check of your home, sleep space, car, and workspace. Do you like the way it smells, looks, feels? Pick one area and do something about it. If it helps you feel energized in your day, then it is necessary.

CHAPTER NINE

SLEEP

"The amount of sleep required for the average person is five minutes more."

– Wilson Mizener

I hope this chapter brings you great sleep (but not until after you have finished reading it!). By now it should be clear to you that the healthy, rested life is unlike some of the go-harder routines that are frequently encouraged and marketed to us. The rested life is one of balance. And at the heart of keeping that balance is spending one-third of our time in intense recovery from the other two-thirds of our time in which we are active. That recovery time, universally needed by us all, is sleep.

There's a lot of machismo that flies around when sleep is discussed. Tell someone you wake by 6:00 a.m. to start your routine, and you're bound to find another proudly boasting about how they started their day at 4:30 a.m. But unless they were in bed by at least 9:30 the previous evening, they are only cheating themselves.

We are so absorbed with productivity and results that we forego the benefits that can actually happen overnight from a good night's rest.

You may be beyond the days of pulling off all-nighters, but cheating yourself that hour or two on either end of your slumber has significant effects. The CDC now defines sleep deprivation as two or more consecutive nights of receiving less than seven hours of sleep. Yes, you read that right. Most people already do this on a regular basis! The March 4, 2011, edition of *Morbidity and Mortality Weekly Report* (yes, that's a real magazine, and yes, I have read it), states that, on average, more than 35% of us sleep less than seven hours a day. Almost 38% of us have fallen asleep unintentionally in the last month, and almost 5% of us have "nodded off" or fallen asleep while driving in the last month. This is scary!

Consider the 1989 Exxon Valdez oil spill; eleven million gallons of crude oil spilled from the hull of a tanker. Crude oil is still evident on the Alaskan coastline to this day. Or consider the 1979 partial nuclear meltdown on Three Mile Island in which an uncertain amount of radioactive material was released into the atmosphere. Or, finally, consider the 1986 Chernobyl Disaster, in which thirty-one people died in the incident itself and thousands (if not millions) of lives are still affected by the radioactive material released. What do these, and many other tragic and costly incidents that happen daily, have in common? Sleep deprivation was a contributing factor. Studies have repeatedly shown that we can't just "get by" with a lack of sleep.

Sleep is the primary supporting element to each of the four sources of energy in our life. I say sleep is just as important as oxygen—we would certainly die without it. We physically suffer from a lack of sleep, losing alertness, coordination, and our ability to fight disease. There are also strong links to poor sleep and cardiovascular issues, diabetes, and obesity. Lack of sleep affects us mentally through poorer decision-making, decreased working memory, and other neural functions. We experience less emotional resilience and a decreased ability to regulate moods. Finally, we suffer spiritually; because when we lack sleep, we move into a survival mode rather than an purposeful and inspired state of living. If there is only one thing for you to address to make improvements in your life, it is sleep. And if none of that is convincing enough, knowing that a lack of sleep negatively affects the sex drive should cause you to want to get a few more winks at night.

The study of sleep has exploded over the last few decades, and I'd encourage you to check out some of it. If you need just a little more convincing to get the sleep you need, check out this short video by Arianna Huffington,[13] and then come back here for a few pointers on how to improve one of your most vital processes—sleep!

---

[13] bit.ly/HuffingtonSleep—case sensitive.

STEPS TO A GREAT NIGHT'S SLEEP

Environment

Our surroundings have an significant impact on our sleep. Do what you can to control the lighting, sounds, and smells. How do you feel when you get into bed? Do you like the heaviness of a thick blanket or prefer to have as little as possible over you? Does your mattress feel supportive? Does your pillow give you support without causing cramps in the neck? You don't need to spend a fortune to get a good bed, but you ought to experiment a little to help you get the best sleep possible. I contend that because our sleep is so important to who we are, the quality of our mattress should be of great importance to us.

Unplugging

Media has become one of our favorite ways to "wind down" at the end of a day. The tricky part is that you may feel relaxed while doing the screen time, but the brightness from the screen can mess with our pineal gland (which releases melatonin that helps us sleep), and the mental stimulation from the content may actually keep you from your best transition to a great night's sleep. Instead, let's replace it with something that is actually relaxing. Rather than doing screen time, I suggest taking a hot shower or bath, sipping some herbal tea, reading for enjoyment, listening to relaxing music, or lighting a calming candle such as lavender. These habits will reward us at the end of our days and allow us to move to a relaxing sleep without overstimulation.

Earlier in the book, we talked about the anxiety we experience when we have been away from our phone. This is well demonstrated when we go to bed. In order to help us feel secure, many of us put our phones right next to our bed at night. I suggest we try to change that habit. At least thirty minutes before you go to bed, consider removing yourself from all electronics and don't allow them in the bedroom. Place the phone in a place that you can still hear the ringer in the case of an emergency, but physically make the separation from it. This will undoubtedly feel strange to some of you at first, and maybe even cause more anxiety the first few nights. But eventually your physical separation from the devices at night will help you make a mental separation from them. This will allow you to embrace the relaxing "me time" before heading off to bed.

Exercise

Every parent knows that exercise helps us sleep, because what is better for preparing your child for bed than taking them to the pool, or sending them out to bounce on the trampoline to help them get the wiggles out?

The National Sleep Foundation has shown that exercising for 150 minutes a week has significant impact on one's sleep. Additionally, the better sleep we have, the better our exercise routine is the following day. It's a positive feedback loop that ought not be ignored! What's a great way to get the best sleep? Exercise. An excellent way to improve your workout? Sleep!

Mental Preparation

Don't take your stresses to your bedroom. Well before you head off to bed, reconcile relationships that you can reconcile. That may be with your spouse, your child, or maybe even a coworker. You may even want to write a card or send an encouraging e-mail to mend a relationship. Say "I'm sorry," even if you don't think you should so that you can go to bed without anxieties.

I told you that I like to start my day off by reminding myself what I have to be grateful for, and you know, it's not a bad way to finish off a day either. It's a great way to release your day and give yourself the permission to disconnect from the world through sleep.

Intake

What foods we eat, when, and how much has a surprising effect on how well we sleep. The first thing to know is that too much food late in the day negatively affects our sleep. Our bodies' sleep processes are distracted from rest and repair as we digest our food. Try not to eat anything after eight p.m. This gives your body an opportunity to "fast" between your last meal and your breakfast. Your body can better utilize the extra energy to restore and repair functions instead of digesting a whole tub of ice cream!

You shouldn't drink too much before heading to bed, either. And what you drink is just as important. Coffee and sodas are obvious sources of caffeine to be avoided, but watch out for the less obvious sources, such as chocolate, tea, and the decaffeinated drinks (decaf coffee often contains up to sixteen milligrams of caffeine). Cut out the caffeine at least six hours before bedtime.

Alcohol presents a unique situation when it comes to sleep. Many people like to drink alcohol to help them fall asleep, which it does. But alcohol has also been shown to wake you up through the night, result in a less restful sleep, and cause headaches, night sweats, and nightmares. If you drink alcohol at night, be sure to keep it in moderation, and add a glass of water to help dilute the negative effects and aid in its digestion.

RHYTHM

Our bodies operate on, and actually crave, rhythm. You may have a free-spirited, go-with-the-flow personality, but your body appreciates pattern. Most all living things have what is called a circadian rhythm. At its most basic level, it is the twenty-four-hour daily cycle. But it gets even more detailed than that. At its next level are the three eight-hour cycles. This is evident in that people sleep an average of eight hours per twenty-four hours, and our bodies like to go to bed and wake at fairly regular times. But did you know that there are cycles while we are awake? Do you feel, like I often do, that lull that occurs in the early afternoon? This is all part of our natural pattern.

By acknowledging that our bodies go through such a cycle, we can help ourselves prepare for our next phase. For example, you can do things like go for a jog, take a brief nap, and eat a healthy, light lunch to help you through that afternoon lag. Likewise, I recommend starting to prepare ourselves for nighttime sleep immediately following dinner. While there are various events that happen in our evenings, we can begin to be conscious that we are moving toward bedtime.

The first step is to choose an appropriate bedtime. While it can be fun to occasionally binge-watch a Netflix show, we have to be aware of how this affects the following day. So the best way to determine a proper bedtime at the end of the day is to consider what an ideal morning will be for you. Bedtime is not just about finally crashing and checking out today; it is much more about you tomorrow! If you know you must be at work by 8:00 a.m., how much prep time do you need? What is your commute? How much time would you like to spend on breakfast? Will you read, pray, or write in your journal in the morning? How much exercise will you fit in? One of the saddest things we do is sabotage a day before it has begun by not carefully determining when we will go to bed and do what it takes to get ourselves there. Bedtime comes every night—it's no surprise. So let's make it great.

Begin to think of your day as winding down following dinner. Then, figure out for yourself—what is your "warm glass of milk?" What things can you do tonight to prepare for your tomorrow (set out your clothes, prepare your breakfast, set the coffee maker, get your study materials or office supplies ready to go). Cherish your sleeping time and make it great—because it affects everything about who you are!

> *"Early to bed, early to rise, makes a man healthy, wealthy, and wise."*
>
> – Benjamin Franklin

CHAPTER SUMMARY

The rested life is one you uniquely balance. And at the heart of keeping that balance is spending one-third of our time in intense recovery from the other two-thirds of our time in which we are active. That recovery time, universally needed by us all, is sleep. The CDC now defines sleep deprivation as two or more consecutive nights of receiving less than seven hours of sleep. Yes, you read that right. Sleep is the primary supporting element to each of the four sources of energy in our life. I say sleep is just as important as oxygen. There are five things to consider to getting a great night's sleep: environment, unplugging, exercise, mental preparation, and intake. It's also important to know that our bodies operate on, and actually crave, rhythm. You may have a free-spirited, go-with-the-flow personality, but your body appreciates pattern. Most living things have what is called a circadian rhythm. By acknowledging that our bodies go through such a cycle, we can help ourselves prepare for our next phase. Cherish your sleeping time and make it great—because it affects everything about who you are!

ACTION STEPS

- Choose an appropriate bedtime. The best way to determine this is to consider what an ideal morning will be for you tomorrow.
- Start to pay attention to your body's natural rhythm and cycles. Keep a journal to note when you feel lulls throughout the day, what your sleep patterns are, and how you feel.
- Do a check of the five steps to a great night's sleep and see where you need to make a few changes to maximize your sleep and give your body the rest it so desperately needs.

CHAPTER TEN

FLOW

"The only pride of her workday was not that it had been lived, but that it had been survived. It was wrong, she thought, viciously wrong that one should be forced to say that about any hour of one's life."

– Ayn Rand

A s you close out this book, you likely have a lot of ideas on how you can enhance your energy level by improving your rest ethic. In fact, you may even feel a sense of being overwhelmed. I hope to help you with that by introducing you to the concept of flow.

Flow is simply this: challenge (internal or external demand) and skill (knowledge, energy, physical ability, and resources) moving proportionately together to provide the greatest fulfillment and success. It is a place of high production and just enough stress so that we can respond to that demand. I believe we are all looking for this place of flow in our lives.

In a business sense, flow is when production meets demand. Profits are up because demand is at your company's capacity to

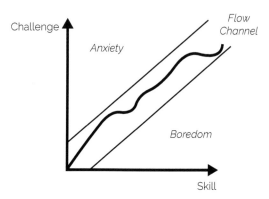

"Flow" concept by Mihaly Csikszentmihalyi.
Drawn by Senia Maymin.

produce (skill), and your system is not stressed to meet the demand (challenge). Life is good. In a sports sense, flow is having a great time performing because you have the ability to make the plays that are required to compete well in the game and your competitor is equally as good, thus providing sufficient challenge.

When we don't have flow, we fall into either anxiety or boredom. As we talked about earlier in the book, anxiety occurs when demand is beyond one's own perceived ability. In other words, when the challenge exceeds skill, we stress. The opposite occurs when we reverse the factors. When our skill far exceeds our demand, we can experience boredom and apathy. A healthy life is lived in flow, where one has the appropriate challenge to match their own skills, providing them a sense of contentment.

To illustrate this further, imagine a garden hose. It looks pretty good when there is great flow coming out of it. The hose itself will represent our skill capacity. The volume of water represents the demand or challenge that we have on us. When the challenge (water) is increased too high, the flow is not as fluid and fulfilling. In fact, the water demonstrates our stress as it sprays uncontrollably. We see this when we restrict the space in which the water can come through by putting a nozzle on the hose or our thumb over the end. Less water comes out, and it comes out in a forceful manner. Our lives are similar when our skill capacity doesn't match the demand that is on us. Physically, mentally, emotionally, and spiritually, we sense this in our lives, and it becomes an energy deficit through stress.

We can use the same idea to find our flow when it comes to work and rest. Imagine a graph with work on one axis and rest on the other. When we work on managing our physical, mental, emotional, and spiritual energies, we basically increase our skill set and increase our adaptability and ability to do more great work. Studies have shown that we are healthier, and actually more productive, when we take regular breaks. Research on rest and taking breaks will reveal a plethora of information and proposed models. I happen to like the Pomodoro model myself. When the amount of work we do moves proportionately with the amount of rest we take, we are in our sweet spot—our flow.

Let's reverse this metaphor for a moment. If your hose is much bigger than the flow going through it, the water comes out more like a trickle. That is, when your skill and energy capacity exceeds the demand that is on your life, you can often feel less than significant, even apathetic. Research reveals to us that our performance rises with the amount of arousal we have for the task (Yerkes-Dodson law). At least to a point. Once a certain level of arousal is hit, your personal effectiveness lessens, and if the stress/arousal continues, you actually become less effective in spite of trying your best. Ideally, you want to try to stay in that sweet spot where you're working and living productively, but not so much that you are exhausted, are tired, and start to notice things slipping. That being said, if we do not receive an arousing challenge, we are more likely to grow indifferent and not perform very well. This is why incentivizing mundane tasks can be an effective motivator.

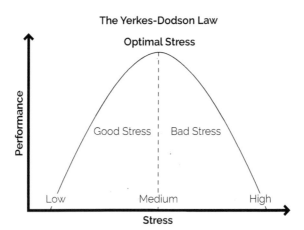

Operating in flow is a beautiful thing, and we feel most like ourselves when we are in flow. It is ideal for us to operate the majority of our time in flow.

There are healthy places of moving outside of flow—for example, trying out a new hobby that piques our interest, like hiking on a new trail, building a new model, or learning a different language. A hobby does not demand production, and is done to be fulfilling and interesting as skills and knowledge are developed. Alternately, it is appropriate that we also have times to do things with low challenge that are well within our skills—such as driving an automobile, because safety demands that we are able to do so with mastery. Thus, automobiles and roads are not designed for challenge and intrigue, but rather made to be driven safely with the least amount of skill necessary.

Our bodies are even designed to operate rhythmically, both on and off. Our brain cells fire and then enter into what is called the refractory period, a rest time, before they can fire again. Cell division has within its process a period of recovery before the division process happens again. And we all know that nightly we must go to sleep. It is just as important that we sometimes turn off as it is that we turn on!

My desire in writing this book is that we will live more aware of the rest that we need in all areas of our lives and be able to make intentional decisions protecting this precious need. There is no shortage of authors writing about the peaks we experience, best practices for improving ourselves, how to produce more, how to impress others, and how to operate in constant demand all in the name of getting more. A lot of this is good stuff, but it sometimes fails to acknowledge that life is not about moving from peak to peak to peak. Life is oscillating. That is, life moves in rhythm. Between those peaks are valleys, and it is important that we know how to be just as intentional in the valleys as we are in the peaks.

Recognizing that life is rhythmic means that on a large time scale, we operate in seasons. There is a time for everything, and everything has its time. So while you may have a number of changes you'd like to make after reading this book, I encourage you to select two to four of the most impactful ones to put your focus on. Maybe you have just one goal in each area: physical, mental, emotional, and spiritual. Set deadlines to your goals, get others involved, and get after it. Then move on to the next goal. You may choose to set goals for different levels of your life. Maybe you have a goal for finding seasons of rest and recovery for your entire life. Perhaps you have plans for growth and challenges along with recovery time in the year ahead. And you should have goals for how to find your flow each day. You may find that you have to revisit one of your goals in a season down the road. That is okay—we are dynamic people, and thus this is not a fix-it-and-forget-it cookbook to make a better you. Finding our flow is a push and pull. It's an illusion to imagine you will always be in the sweet spot. It's more peaks and valleys, but the peaks and valleys can be less intense. You have to be intentional to have flow in your life. It's so easy to get distracted, so set that as your intention. The intention is to live a life this way; to marry work with rest and recovery. Setting this intention is an amazing thing, and amazing things come from that.

So hold on to this book, and do some research on some of the topics that have been discussed—and over time you and I both will continue to have our fullest lives and reach our greatest potentials.

My hope is that after having read this book, you recognize just how important it is to have a strong rest ethic. My wish is that you feel inspired to make a few changes in your life to create one, and by doing so, be a more authentic version of you and inspire others to do the same. After all, the reason I wrote this book to begin with is because I needed to learn all of this stuff myself.

CHAPTER SUMMARY

Flow is simply this: challenge (internal or external demand) and skill (knowledge, energy, physical ability, and resources) moving proportionately together to provide the greatest fulfillment and success. It is a place of high production and just enough stress that we can respond to the demand. We can use the same idea to find our flow when it comes to work and rest. I believe we are all looking for this place of flow in our lives. When we don't have flow, we fall into either anxiety or boredom. Our bodies are even designed to operate rhythmically, both on and off. Life is oscillating. That is, life moves in a rhythm between peaks are valleys, and it is important that we know how to be just as intentional in the valleys as we are in the peaks. Recognizing that life is rhythmic means that on a large time scale, we operate in seasons. Finding our flow is a push and pull and requires our intention. So hold on to this book, and do some research on some of the topics that have been discussed. Over time you and I both will continue to have our fullest lives and reach our greatest potentials.

ACTION STEPS

- Select the most important and urgent goals you now have after reading this book and choose to make a concerted effort to address those two to four matters.
- Set deadlines to your goals, get others involved, and go after them.
- Set a date to revisit your goals in the future. We are dynamic, so it's okay to revisit and refocus goals as we go.

ACKNOWLEDGEMENTS

An incredible life is made up of incredible people. I'm fortunate to have some incredible people in my life that I'd like to acknowledge.

To my wife, Treva—my best friend, confidant and soulmate—thank you for your love, faith, and belief in me. From our first date you made me want to become more and live a bigger, richer life. Looking back at that first date, I know that we have. I am truly blessed to have you in my life. You've helped me become a better man. I can't imagine sharing a life with anyone else.

To my son, Matthew, you are such an inspiration to me, I can hardly explain it in words but I'll try. You help remind me that just about anything really is possible. You inspire me to become the best dad and person I can, knowing that the best way to help teach you is to be a living example. You remind me that I need to play more, laugh more, and play more video games. You are absolutely a gift from God who one day will be a gift to the world.

To my mom and dad, thank you for helping instill such a great work ethic in me. You both are amazing examples of what commitment to each other, combined with hard work, can bring to a life. Both of you came from humble beginnings and against the odds have created a business, family, and life that few people ever achieve. Thanks for being such role models and being so supportive and patient because I know Andrew and I pushed every "parent-button" possible on our way to adulthood—and occasionally in adulthood. Having my own son has made me understand where your gray hair has come from! Love you both!

To my brother, Andrew, and sister-in-law, Terri, thanks for being such an example of how to juggle several businesses, four amazing kids, and four dogs and still have time for a life! Andrew, I am amazed at the man you've become and could not be more proud of what you've achieved as well as how you live your life on your terms. You've been an inspiration for this book.

To my mother-in-law, Theresa, you helped me understand what it's like to face incredible life adversity and come out on top. Your love, faith, and humor are a testament to what a person can become when they overcome the challenges of life. In your quiet way, you truly left the world a better place. Love you and miss you, Nonie!

To my sister and brothers-in-law: Marcella and Todd, Tracey and Steven, Doug and Lisa and Shelley and Howard, thank you for your years of support, fun, laughs, and just great times. Not to mention all the nephews and nieces!

To my childhood friends, Terry, Chris, Mike, and Leeann, I appreciate your friendship and support over the years and I look forward to so many great years ahead.

To Dr. Frank Sovinsky, Cathy Sovinsky, Dr. Cecile Thackeray, and Dr. Doug Sea, just thanking you would be an understatement. Through your guidance and support, you have helped shape the doctor, entrepreneur, and person that I've become. What you've helped create and given me simply can't be paid back—but I will be paying it forward, starting with this book. Thank you all for being such incredible mentors, leaders, and people. Thanks also to all of my friends and colleagues in the DC Mentors tribe that have been so much more than colleagues. You all have been inspirations and are, in my opinion, of the highest calibre in our profession.

To Jennifer Welsh, who opened my eyes to truly understand self-care and the illusion of living a one-sided life (all work and no play!). Your insight and intuition have been a key to unlocking the best version of me. Thank you!

To Dr. Arlan Fuhr and Judi Fuhr, thank you for creating and helping to teach me the art and clinical skills of Activator Methods. Dr. Fuhr, you truly are a great C.E.O (Chief Encouraging Officer) and an example of an entrepreneur making a worldwide impact. Thank you both for your trust, belief, and the opportunity to be a part of the Activator family all of these years.

To the patients I've been entrusted with over many years, I thank you for your trust. Being your doctor is something I hold in the highest regard. Thank you for teaching me about how best to help you.

To the dedicated team that I've been blessed to work with: Anna, Heather, Jess, Nicole, and Mary. Together, you have all helped and touched the lives of so many. Your level of commitment and professionalism is inspiring.

Finally I'd like to thank Jeremy Brown and his team at Throne Publishing for their help in bringing *The Rest Ethic* from an idea to the book you know hold in your hands. It has been a long road to completion and I am so thankful for your patience, professionalism, and exceptional publishing experience. Thank you!

Sincerely,

Dr. Sean Orr

ABOUT THE AUTHOR

Dr. Sean Orr is a dad, husband, chiropractor, speaker, trainer and author. He and his team have developed one of the most successful chiropractic practices in Canada and have helped thousands of patients reach their health goals. Dr. Orr has also  taught chiropractors from across North America and the world through his role as a Clinical Instructor for Activator Methods. When he is not engaged in the work that he loves, he is with the people he loves—his wife and son, his family and close friends. Dr. Orr and his family live in beautiful Stratford, Ontario Canada. Every day he does his best to be more, have more and do less.